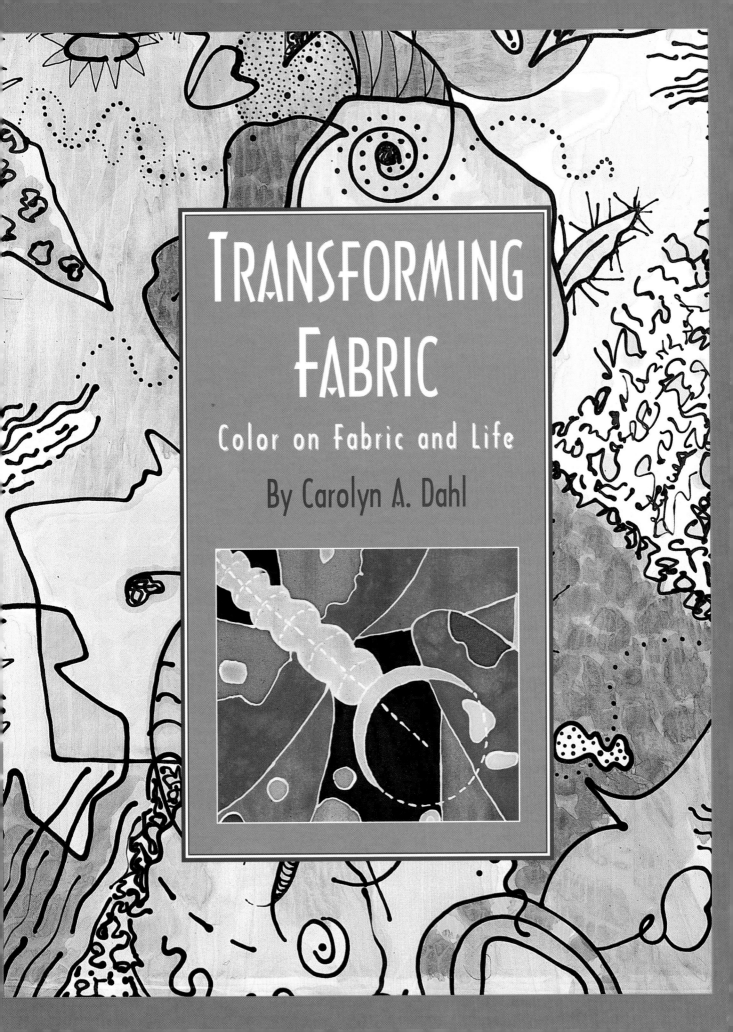

TRANSFORMING FABRIC

Color on Fabric and Life

By Carolyn A. Dahl

Located in Paducah, Kentucky, the American Quilter's Society (AQS) is dedicated to promoting the accomplishments of today's quilters. Through its publications and events, AQS strives to honor today's quiltmakers and their work—and inspire future creativity and innovation in quiltmaking.

Library of Congress Catalog-in-Publication Data

Dahl, Carolyn A.
   Trasforming fabric : color on fabric and life / by Carolyn A. Dahl.
      p. cm.
   ISBN 1–57432–700–3
   1. Dyes and dyeing—Textile fibers. 2. Dyes and dyeing. Domestic.
   3. Textile painting. I. Title.
TT853.D34   1997
746.6—dc21   97–39715
                                                                    CIP

COVER DESIGN
TERRY WILLIAMS

BOOK DESIGN
STAN GREEN / GREEN GRAPHICS

ILLUSTRATION
JUSTIN C. GREEN

Additional copies of this book may be ordered from
American Quilter's Society, P.O. Box 3290, Paducah, KY 42002–3290
@$29.95
Add $2.00 for postage & handling

Liability Disclaimer:

The author and publisher of this book bear no responsibility for any physical injury, destruction of property, or any other loss, damage, liability, or claim resulting from the use of products and procedures described in this book, whether used properly or improperly.
The information contained in this publication is presented in good faith and is reliable to the best of our knowledge. No warranty is given, nor results guaranteed, since the conditions of use are beyond our control. The author and publisher assume no responsibility for the use of this data.

DEDICATION

To my husband, Thomas Perry,
whose constant love and support
keep me true to who I am meant to be.

ACKNOWLEDGMENTS

To Don Wiener at PRO Chemical and Dye who reviewed the dye chapter for technical accuracy and who has so many times over the years helped me understand dyeing from a chemist's rather than an artist's perspective.

To the many suppliers who provided whatever assistance I needed, to W. Finley Klass at Testfabrics Inc. for help in my cloth research, to Jane McCauley for her helpful editing, to Terry Williams for his beautiful cover, to Stan Green for the creative layout, and to Meredith Schroeder, my publisher, for her gracious patience.

To the artists in this book who generously shared their techniques and photos of their beautiful works.

To Lisa Selzman, my writer friend, who always believed in this book and who taught me patience with the writing process.

To my writing group, Betty Allen-Trembly, Heidi Straube, and Helen Weekes, for their insightful comments, the hours of listening, and their constant encouragement.

To Wanda Ostrom an early teacher who encouraged and mentored my direction before I even knew what it was.

To my mother Irene Helen Holmes for allowing me to dream my own dreams and always supporting my choices.

To my stepfather Archie Holmes for teaching me about taking risks as he brought wild horses home from South Dakota, took flying lessons, and worked in the jungles of Africa. He fought against cancer bravely, but lost with dignity and peace during the writing of this book.

To my sister Candace Holmes-Boser who holds our family together with her love and humor, and who influences so many young lives with her dedicated and caring teaching.

To my Swedish grandmother, Ellen Albertina Dahl, for the memories of velvet dresser scarves, dyed silk stocking rugs, tins of colored buttons and beads, coffee-filled winters cutting cloth into strips, and the summer sound of the old loom beating out rag rugs. Your love of textiles lives in me and this book.

To Victoria Faoro, director of the Museum of American Quilter's Society, who asked me to write this book. Without her posing the question, it would never have entered my mind, nor exist now.

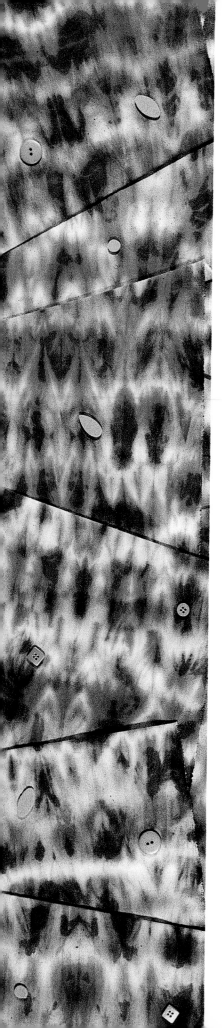

CONTENTS

INTRODUCTION 1

CHAPTER 1: THE CLOTH: BOWING TO THE WHITE 2

  COTTON: LITTLE "TREE LAMBS" 2

  SILK: QUEEN OF FABRICS 5

  RAYON: ARTIFICIAL SILK 9

  PREPARING FABRIC FOR COLOR 10

CHAPTER 2: THE COLORANTS 12

  EARLY TEXTILE DYES 13

  FIBER REACTIVE DYES 13

  RECIPES FOR DYEING WITH FIBER REACTIVE DYES 16

  FABRIC PAINTS 23

CHAPTER 3: BLACK & WHITE TRANSFORMATIONS 28

  BEGINNER'S PATTERNS 28

CHAPTER 4: BLENDED COLOR PATTERNS 34

  COLOR WASHES 34

  SPRAY DYEING 38

  SPRAY DYEING WITH NEWSPAPER STENCILS 40

CHAPTER 5: NATURE'S PATTERNS 44

  RAIN PATTERNING 44

  LEAF PRINTING 48

  FISH PRINTING AND GYOTAKU 53

  HELIOTROPIC PRINTING 59

CHAPTER 6: SPONGE & HEATED-FOAM PRINTING 64

  SPONGES AND PATTERNS 65

  SPONGING PROCEDURE FOR ANIMAL, CELLULOSE,
  AND SYNTHETIC SPONGES 68

CHAPTER 7: COMPRESSION DYEING 72

  TECHNIQUES 73

  BRAIDING 73

  TWISTING, KNOTTING, AND BINDING 75

  SCRUNCHING 79

  STITCH AND DYE 81

CHAPTER 8: HEAT TRANSFER DYES 86
    HISTORY 86
    IMPORTANT FACTORS 87
    DYE TRANSFER INK STAMP PADS 88
    WAX TRANSFER CRAYONS 92
    TRANSFER MARKER PENS 93
    DYE-SATURATED PAPER SHEETS 94
    USED INDUSTRIAL DYE SHEETS 96
    READY-TO-USE TRANSFER PAINT 96
    POWDERED DISPERSED DYES 97

CHAPTER 9: SELF-DESIGNED STAMPS 98
    DESIGNING YOUR STAMP 100

CHAPTER 10: DESTRUCTION PATTERNS 106
    DISCHARGE/BLEACH PATTERNS 106
    DEVORÉ OR BURN-OUT TECHNIQUES 113

CHAPTER 11: WAX PATTERNS 116
    DYE PAINTING WITH WAX RESIST 116
    SELECTING THE WAX RESIST 121
    STRETCHING THE FABRIC ON THE FRAME 124
    WAX STAMPING 129

CHAPTER 12: SILK PAINTING 136
    SILK FABRIC 138
    GUTTA 138
    PAINTING TECHNIQUES 142
    SALT EFFECTS 143

CLOSING 146
FOOTNOTES 147
SUPPLY SOURCES 148
INDEX 150
ABOUT THE AUTHOR 153

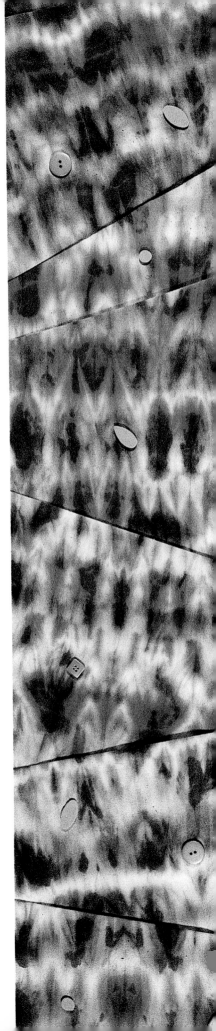

Introduction

This book is about transforming fabric. With dyes, textile paints, and pattern-making techniques the fabric can become anything you desire. But coloring and designing cloth isn't just about what one's hands do, but also where your mind and soul wander during the process. I know that while I work on the cloth, the procedures are also transforming me as an artist and a person.

No art or technique ever exists outside someone's life. It's always connected to a soul. And where there's a soul, there are stories. As I believe that both the technical and personal perspectives are important in understanding a process, this book is a blend of both. I hope you will enjoy my stories as I battle the "dye devils," relate tidbits of dyeing history, connect hotel sewing kits and stitch dyeing, honor my materials, and describe the beautiful in-process moments that only the dyer sees.

To make the technical information easy to use by everyone, whether a beginner or experienced artist, I have organized the chapters as mini-workshops. Each process is introduced and then covered in detailed, step-by-step instructions that can be followed easily without an instructor.

I chose this format because I wanted to err on the side of too much information in the directions, rather than too little. Over the years, I have discovered that success often comes from the details that some directions skip. For example, you may not be able to achieve good results with certain patterns if the author doesn't tell you what type of surface the fabric should rest on (plastic, paper, cloth). Additionally, the more you know, whether about the interaction between paint and plastic or the ingredients in your dye recipes, the more control you'll have over the artistic process and the greater your ability to solve your own technical problems.

Instead of leading you through steps for a finished product, I prefer to focus on developing the skills needed to complete your own projects. I have taught these procedures to quilters, wearable artists, stitchers, painters, basketmakers, weavers, and surface designers who all use the techniques in different ways. If I can provide you with an understanding of the nature of your tools and materials, can help you envision the possibilities and limitations of each technique, show you how the cloth reacts through fabric samples, and then let you dive into the process, your own imagination will come alive.

As most people feel comfortable using fabric paint but less confident about the chemistry of dyes, I have adapted the majority of the dyeing procedures so they will work with one dye type (fiber reactives). After reading the chapter on how the dyes and ingredients work and interact, you will see that all the information condenses into simple recipes that are quickly memorized. You will be able to turn to any one of the many dyeing techniques collected in this book, or combine several together, without having to learn new recipes or store additional supplies once you have the basics in hand. Within a day, or even 1–2 hours, you'll be able to have fabric with the exact color, image, and pattern you want— all without leaving your studio.

How you use this book will depend upon your needs. It can be a means to learn the fundamentals of many techniques, or as a source book for your own experimentation. It can be a work manual, becoming worn and spotted with dye, or an impetus to think about your own life stories in relationship to your craft or art. However you use it, our mutal interest in cloth, paint, and dye will connect us. Your presence has been by my side from the moment the first words hit the paper until the last. Now maybe as you read and use this book, my presence will sit with you. Use it creatively, often, and bravely.

Facing page: *Transformations* by Carolyn Dahl
Fiber reactive dyes with gutta resist on silk, 45" x 72". Photo by Michael McCormick.

Chapter 1

THE CLOTH: BOWING TO THE WHITE

The Japanese philosophy of Naikan suggests that we not only acknowledge the debts owed to people who have helped us, but also to the objects that serve us. Before beginning work, a Japanese artist might bow in reverence to a beautiful brush, or an office worker to a computer. Although I may not physically bow, I agree with the philosophy and am grateful for the materials that are my co-creators.

As a surface designer, my collaborators are the fabric, dyes, paints, and the application tools. Cloth is perhaps the most important component. It is both the raw material that receives the colors, and the final product that goes into the world to become something else. The most widely used fabrics for dyeing and painting are cotton, silk, and viscose rayon. These three give you a wide range of surfaces and weights and can be used with all of the techniques in this book, except the heat transfer process which requires synthetic fabric.

When the cloth arrives in my studio, it is white, unadorned, ready for me to apply color. But I know that every yard contains the invisible fingerprints of growers, scientists, spinners, weavers, and shippers. Sometimes when I unroll a bolt of silk from China, I can even smell the rooms it has passed through. I will never know all the personal stories I'm rinsing away as I prepare the fabric for dyeing, but knowing a little of the fiber's origin and history makes me appreciate the cloth more.

COTTON: LITTLE "TREE LAMBS"

Cotton is the cloth of our land. The United States is second only to China in cotton production. Grown in the southern "cotton belt," it is a homey, comforting fabric. Long a part of our nation's history, we may even remember some facts from our childhood lessons: relative of the hollyhock, requires six months of warm weather, a cotton boll is the seed pod, cotton fibers can be $3/4$" to $1^1/2$" long, and Thomas Edison used cotton thread when he invented the light bulb. Later in life, we may notice that our food contains cottonseed oil, cattle are fed the hulls, paper and rayon are made from the short fibers (linters) clinging to the cotton seed, and folksingers immortalize the destructive boll weevil "just a-looking for a home" in a cotton field.

We've probably all held a cotton boll in our hands and used cotton fabric. After all, cotton has been spun

1-1 Detail *Nuclear Forest #2* by Carolyn Dahl.
Fiber reactive dyes on silk; compression, discharge, and appliqué techniques. Photo by Michael McCormick.

and woven for over 7,000 years. Cotton may even have played a part in Columbus's error. When he arrived in the New World, the natives presented him with cotton thread. As he believed that cotton existed only in India, he was sure this gift proved he had found a sea route to the Far East. [1]

Apparently, cotton had the ability to mislead a lot of early adventurers. In 1350, Sir John Mandeville returned to England after an expedition to India exclaiming over the sheep on branches he had seen. His exact words were "There grew there a wonderful tree which bore tiny lambs on the endes of its branches. These branches were so pliable that they bent down to allow the lambs to feed when they are hungrie." [2] As wool was the main fiber in those days, I suppose it was easy for Sir John to confuse an open, fluffy cotton boll with a handful of wool fleece. Yet even today, the image of "tree lambs" persists in the German word for cotton, *baumwolle*, which translates to "tree wool."

Purchasing Cotton

When selecting cotton fabric for surface design, consider two factors: the surface texture and treatment. Try to match the fabric's weave to your chosen technique. For example, if you want to produce detailed, precise images, you need a smooth, fine surface that won't interrupt your design. However, if your design is loose and free-form, a rougher textured fabric could add interest to a pattern.

The second factor is to avoid purchasing cotton that has any surface finish, such as permanent press; water, stain, or crease resistant; or flameproofing. Many of these finishes are resin coatings that are extremely difficult to remove without strong chemical scouring. Not only do these chemical additives block dye absorption, but they may also weaken the cotton and hasten deterioration by sunlight.

One term you may find on the bolt label that is desirable, however, is mercerization. During this process, the fabric is treated with caustic soda (sodium hydroxide) while being stretched. This causes the twisted, dried

1-2 *Nuclear Forest #2* by Carolyn Dahl. Dyed silkwork.

cotton fiber to become smoother and more light reflective. The process was discovered when John Mercer, an English calico printer, filtered a lye solution through cotton cloth in 1844. Although the process sounds as if it would damage the fiber, he noted that the fabric became more absorbent, easier to dye, stronger, and less prone to shrinking.[3] Most important from a dyer's viewpoint, is that mercerized cotton will yield a 20 to 25 percent deeper color intensity than untreated cotton.

The reflective quality of the color in mercerized versus non-mercerized cotton will also be different. Non-mercerized cotton will dye lighter, and tend to have a matte appearance. Many people find this less-reflective, subdued quality quite beautiful. The colors have a mellow, seasoned look to them. Others, however, feel non-mercerized cotton gives their colors a lifeless quality. They prefer the mercerized cotton with its more reflective and lustrous surface appeal. It's all a matter of personal preference, but something you may want to consider when choosing cotton to dye.

SILK: QUEEN OF FABRICS

Standing before an old crazy quilt, my eye zigzags through colors and stitches but suddenly halts. Before me is something that breaks the heart of every textile artist—a burgundy silk triangle crumbling away. Perhaps this sight, more than any other reason, has discouraged modern quilters from using the "queen of fabrics." Before rejecting silk as a fabric for quilts or fiber works, however, remember that many factors contributed to the deterioration of crazy quilt silk that now can be avoided.

Most of the silks used weren't new, but were often the best sections of someone's already worn clothing—a favorite dress, a tie, or even a family christening gown. Already weakened through years of use, the silks were then stretched on an embroidery hoop and punctured with needles as the decorative stitches were added. Even though the silks were appliquéd to a background fabric, they seldom had the additional support that quilting or batting would have added. Often the

layers were simply tied together. This construction method allowed the already fragile silk pieces to suffer more stretching and pulling during use.

When crazy quilts were made (approximately 1876 to 1930), their makers didn't know much about light damage or fabric preservation. Made as examples of a needleworker's skills (the original art quilt!), they were displayed hanging on walls, covering pianos, or as throws across chairs without any consideraton for incoming light. Today we are acutely aware of the effect of sunlight on textiles and would never subject them to full sunlight or even strong daylight.

The greatest enemy of crazy quilts, though, was the common practice of weighting silks excessively (also known as loading or dynamiting). To make a lightweight silk feel heavier and have a good drape, various types of fillers were added. The most damaging were metallic salts. Black and dark colors, so popular in crazy quilts, often had the highest concentration. These salts did not wash out and eventually caused the fiber to become brittle and crack from the additional weight (silk can absorb more than its own weight of metallic salts). Mistakenly, people think the silk is rotting, when actually it is more resistant than cotton and other fabrics to mildew and mold.

Luckily, the practice of weighting silks heavily is very rare today. If any loading takes place, the law requires that the amounts be carefully controlled to prevent damage, or the silk must be labeled weighted. So if you purchase new silk and do not expose it to direct sunlight, you can avoid many of the problems now apparent in old quilts.

Silk is the longest, strongest, and most resilient of the natural fibers. Benjamin Franklin chose silk for his famous kite. Sky divers used to trust their lives to it as they hurled themselves out of airplanes in parachutes made mostly of silk. I hope quilters will trust it again for their quilts. After all, every fabric deteriorates in time, as does everything in life. We all want our works to last as long as possible, but sometimes we worry so much about the longevity of our objects that we forget they serve the quality of our lives. Visit a museum and look at all the old pottery, textiles, and jewelry. Now look for their makers. We humans are the fragile ones.

The Divine Worm

Chinese empress Hsi-Ling-Shi probably thought that silk did come from heaven. According to legend, she was sitting under a mulberry tree when a silk cocoon splashed into her teacup. The hot liquid softened the cocoon, and a beautiful filament started to unwind. No tea leaves could have predicted what an important discovery the fourteen-year-old empress made that day, nor that China would hold the secret for 3,000 years.

Today the methods of sericulture, the commercial production of silk cocoons, is well known by many countries. However, most of our silk still comes from the Orient, mainly China and Japan. America was involved in sericulture in the past, most notably by the Mormons and Shakers, but all that remains of the industry are a few mulberry trees.

Two types of silk are produced today: silk from the cocoons of silkworms living in the wild and silk from cocoons of domesticated silkworms. The wild silk is difficult to dye (fabric paints work nicely, though), and its coarser texture makes it less adaptable to surface design techniques, so our focus will be on the silk produced from the domesticated silkworm.

The creamy white Bombyx Mori moth produces the best cultivated silk. Once a wild silk moth, it has been domesticated for over 5,000 years and is now extinct in the wild. Even though it has a long lineage, its own life cycle is short—about two months. During that time, however, it passes through four stages: the egg, caterpillar, chrysalis, and adult moth (scientific terms are the ova, larva, pupa, and imago).[4] The story of its transformation is not only interesting, but also important to understanding and appreciating the fiber's characteristics.

Tiny Grains

The eggs, or grains, which have been kept in cold storage approximately six weeks after being laid, are bathed gently in warm water, dried in the air, and kept in incubators for approximately 30 days. In the old days peasants who raised the silkworms in their homes used to keep the eggs warm by placing them under their pillows, in manure beds, behind stoves, or even in special pouches women wore against their breasts.[5] The eggs are so tiny (pin head size) that 40,000 eggs weigh no more than an ounce. No wonder two monks were able to steal the carefully guarded secret of sericulture from the Chinese in A.D. 552 by hiding the tiny eggs in the hollows of their walking sticks. At least that's how legend says the emperor of Constantinople received them and sericulture spread to the world.

Cultivated Caterpillars

When the eggs hatch, delicate white silkworms about $1/16$" to $1/4$" long appear. Although they are caterpillars, technically, they are always referred to as silkworms. Despite their tiny size (often picked up on the end of a painting brush), the little silkworms are ready to eat 10,000 times their initial weight. Although they will eat cabbage and lettuce, their favorite food is the leaves of the mulberry tree, which produces the highest quality of silk.

For the next three to four weeks, the silkworms' only purpose in life is to eat, grow, sleep, and shed their skin four times. During this part of the growing cycle, the silkworms must be given careful attention. Their mulberry leaves should be crisp, cool, free of pollutants, and dry, as wet leaves will kill them. Their cages must be cleaned constantly and they don't like odors. According to some sources, Chinese women who tend the silkworms may not even wear makeup, and certainly not smoke or eat garlic. In fact, if the silkworms refuse to construct cocoons at the proper time, but want to go on eating, the grower can use a plate of fried onions to make them lose their appetites and begin spinning cocoons.[6]

Above all, silkworms demand quiet. They must not be disturbed when sleeping or eating. According to folklore, a noisy thunderstorm could so upset the worms that they

A. Silkworms feasting on mulberry leaves. **B.** A silkworm begins to spin a cocoon inside an "apartment" made from a cardboard tube. **C.** The silk moth secretes an alkaline liquid to create an escape hole, which breaks the long silk filaments of the cocoon. **D.** The newly emerged silk moth has a beautiful creamy color, like undyed silk. Home sericulture and photography by Connie Elliot.

would immediately stop eating, and would fail to develop properly. So some poor soul was elected to go out into the lightning and rain with a hot coal to drive away the evil spirits disturbing the worms.[7]

It amuses me to imagine all the workers tiptoeing and whispering around the silkworms. I remember the little tree I had on my patio that was a host to another species of caterpillars one summer. The sound of them munching through the night kept me awake in my upstairs bedroom. How quiet can 300,000 silkworms be, chewing mulberry leaves at a rate of five feedings a day? Apparently it's the alien nature of certain noises that disturbs them, just as the noise of gnawing caterpillars kept me awake.

Silken Cloaks

Soon the silkworms stop eating, turn a transparent, pinkish flesh color, and begin to act restless. Having reached their full length of 3 to $3^1/2$", they begin to search for an object on which to spin their cocoons. Once they begin bobbing their heads from side to side in a rearing motion, the caretakers know it is time to move the worms to individual cubicles.

As soon as the silkworm is placed in its compartment, it begins to wrap itself in a protective cocoon to initiate its metamorphosis into a chrysalis. Working in a figure-eight pattern, the worm ejects two filaments from a hole in its lower jaw called the spinneret. One filament is a barely visible protein strand called fibroin; the other is a glutinous substance called sericin, or silk gum. The two filaments merge and harden when they are exposed to the air.

Within 24 hours, the worm is hidden from view but continues to spin inside the cocoon for three to four days. It is estimated that the caterpillar spins 20 to 30 layers of filaments or approximately 1,000 to 4,000 feet of unbroken filament. As it gets tired, the fibers at the center of the cocoon will be weaker. Finally exhausted, the silkworm rests, wrapped in its silken cloak. The cocoon must not be disturbed as the transformation inside takes place.

Chrysalis Dreams

In about eight days the silkworm will have remade itself inside and out. Shedding its caterpillar skin, it becomes a brown shell filled with yellow liquid (the chrysalis), which develops into an adult moth. If the moth were allowed to emerge, however, the long filament of the cocoon would be broken into short threads where the moth escaped. Unfortunately, the chrysalis is destroyed (or stifled), usually by warming or steaming the cocoon.

In home-raised cocoons, where the silk production is small, the cocoon can be unreeled when freshly spun with the live chrysalis inside. Some silk filament is allowed to remain around the chrysalis, so it can grow into a moth and emerge unharmed. In large scale silk production, however, the cocoons will be stored before unwinding the silk, so the chrysalides' development must be halted. Being of a tender heart, I like the sentiment in this Haiku poem:

> *Sleeping in its bed*
> *Of silk,*
> *The caterpillar*
> *Dreams the butterfly.*[8]

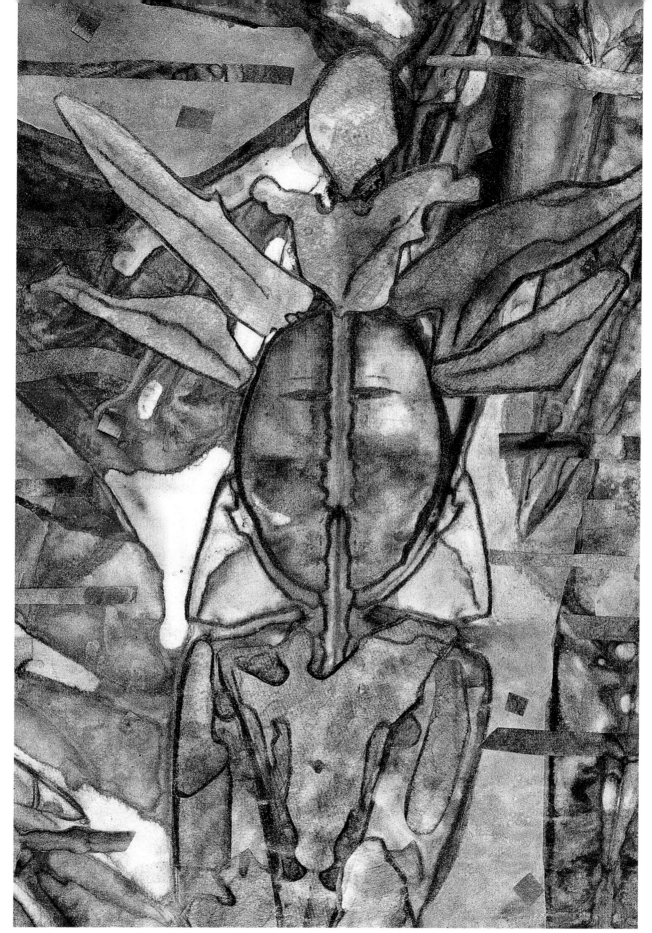

1-3 *Nature Spirit* by Carolyn Dahl. Thickened dyes, fabric paint, collage on silk.
Photo by Maria Davila, National Photographic Lab.

White Moths

Out of each batch some cocoons, often called queen cocoons regardless of sex, must be allowed to mature and produce the next generation of moths. Since some of each sex must be collected, the cocoons are sorted by weight (the females are heavier than the males). When the creamy white moths emerge, they unfold their useless wings, and mate. The female lays anywhere from 300 to 600 eggs and dies within a week.

Unlike a butterfly that has a proboscis to take in nectar and water, the silk moth has no means of nourishment. It does not have a digestive system and cannot drink or chew. Perhaps that is why the silkworm's appetite is so voracious. It must store nutrients to be passed along to the moth so it can survive long enough to complete its short life cycle.[9] Perhaps the "caterpillar dreaming the butterfly" was not so unfortunate after all.

Divine Threads

When they are ready to be unwound, the cocoons are placed in hot water to soften the sericin (glue) so the beginning of the silk filament can be found. Because the strand is so delicate, the filaments of five or six cocoons are unwound together onto one bobbin. Even this many cocoons produce a very fine strand. To make more usable thread, six or seven bobbins must be twisted together, the number depending on the type of silk to be woven. When you realize that it takes about 110 cocoons for the silk in a tie and 1,500 for a dress, you can understand why silk fabric is so precious and why I call the worm divine.

RAYON: ARTIFICIAL SILK

Rayon was developed as a silk substitute by a Frenchman. When a disease threatened to destroy whole colonies of European silkworms, Louis Pasteur was hired in 1878 to solve the mystery of the black and dying worms. A pupil of his, a Frenchman named Count Hilaire de Chardonnet, was also studying silkworms.[10]

Perhaps because he believed that the whole silk industry was on the brink of extinction, Chardonnet hoped to duplicate the silkworm's product using chemicals. After all, silk wasn't really a fiber, but a secretion. It took the shape of a filament when the worm forced the liquid through a hole, or spinneret. Once out of the silkworm's body, the shaped secretion hardened in the air. Chardonnet knew that a spinneret could be mimicked in metal, but finding the right chemical combination to duplicate the secretion was more difficult.

In 1884 Chardonnet succeeded by dissolving nitrocellulose in alcohol and ether. He opened a factory to produce his artificial silk, which it was called for many years. In 1924 it was given a new name, rayon, because it described the early, lustrous, almost metallic fabric as it reflected the sun's rays. Chardonnet is credited as the inventor of rayon, the first man-made fiber. But he really should share the honor with the silkworm who was the source for the idea. Chardonnet admitted he had never really reproduced the silkworm's product, but he did introduce a new fiber to the world. Today the processes for producing rayon have changed greatly. The buyer can select lustrous fabrics that resemble silk, dull rayons that mimic cotton, sheers that look like chiffon, or rayons as heavy as satins. Mixed with other fibers, rayon has come into its own and finally out of the shadow of silk.

Purchasing Rayon

There are two types of rayon—viscose rayon which the fiber-reactive dyes used in this book will color, and acetate rayon which they will not. Both rayons come from cellulosic materials (wood pulp or cotton linters) but are processed differently. Viscose rayon is produced through an alkali process; it gets its name because the resulting solution is thick, like honey, before being forced through the metal spinneret and extruded as a fiber. Acetate rayon is produced by an acid process, specifically acetic acid, for which it is named.

Unfortunately, the labels on fabric bolts do not identify whether the rayon is viscose or acetate. If you order your fabric from a dye supplier you will always get the dyeable rayon. If you purchase your fabric elsewhere, ask for a sample. Take it home and give it the burn test. Viscose rayon will produce a feathery ash that smells like burnt paper. Acetate rayon will leave a charred, bead-like residue, that has a slight vinegar smell (the acetic acid in its process). If you are still in doubt, try dyeing $1/8$ yard before purchasing the full amount.

Whether you chose to work with "tree lambs," "the divine worm," or the "sun's rays," try to develop a respect for the fiber. Cloth isn't just woven threads. Like the incense fragrance that remains in the textiles I bought in a Mexican market years ago, each piece of fabric you use has a history to it. It came from a plant, an animal, a worm, or a synthetic solution. Years of industrial inventions, scientific research, and loving care were required to bring it to you. I think it's worth a little bow of recognition.

PREPARING FABRIC FOR COLORING

Even if you've purchased fabrics free of specific surface treatments, they will still contain some type of sizing added for consumer appeal. To remove these additives and any other impurities, the fabrics must be thoroughly washed before coloring. Although you can hand wash a small amount of fabric, larger amounts are more easily done in the machine. If the fabric lengths are very long, divide them into smaller pieces to avoid knotting (especially with silk).

As the fabric will shrink during the washing process, always allow an extra 1" to 2" per yard. Most fabrics won't shrink more than this amount. However, after a silk pongee lost 3" per yard during washing, I now do a test sample first whenever I have limited yardage or am working on a commission. Whatever your fabric, do not add fabric softener to the wash, or use fabric softener sheets in the dryer. Your purpose in washing the fabric is to remove, and to avoid adding, any chemicals that may interfere with the colorant's bonding with the fiber.

Washing Cotton

1. Set your machine for a long wash cycle with hot water. Cotton is a very durable fabric (the Army uses it for their uniforms) and can withstand machine agitation and high temperatures as its fibers are stronger wet than dry.

2. Use a laundry detergent or a commercial scouring agent from a dye supplier, such as Synthrapol. If using Synthrapol, mix about 2 teaspoons of it with 2 teaspoons PRO Dye Activator (soda ash) per gallon of wash water (140° to 200°F).[11]

3. After washing and rinsing, either line or machine dry the fabric at a cotton setting.

4. Iron fabric on a cotton setting, using steam if necessary. Cotton is not as elastic as other natural fibers and wrinkles considerably after the sizing is removed during washing. Although some dyers believe ironing closes the fabric pores, I find that the wrinkles interfere with certain patterning processes and block dye penetration. So I prefer to remove them as completely as possible. Once ironed, the fabric is ready to be colored.

If you do not intend to use your fabric right away, avoid making creases by folding it. Instead roll the fabric on a tube. If the fabric must be stored for a long time, don't put it in a damp, dark environment that might cause mildew to develop.

Although cotton fabric with sizing in it is more susceptible, mildew can also form on clean fiber. Mildew is a parasitic fungus that changes cellulose to sugar, on which it then feeds. Cotton is 85 to 90 percent cellulose and absorbs moisture quickly but dries slowly; so it is very prone to the fungus. Be sure to store your fabric in a light, airy spot.

Washing Silk

For years I hand washed all my silk until a banquet-size tablecloth changed my mind. Usually I wash the silk as yardage, paint the design, and then have the pieces seamed together later. But a clever interior designer wanted the waxed floral pattern I was to paint to cross over the seams. So she thought she had to arrive with the tablecloth completely constructed—all 20 yards of it. As the silk could not be taken apart again, but did have to be washed before painting, I tried to solve the problem as best I could. Lacking a large sink, I chose my biggest plastic garbage can, my garden hose, and a bare patch in my backyard. After carrying buckets of hot water from the house and filling the container with additional hose water, I plunged the lightweight silk into the sudsy water.

At the first swish, I knew I was in trouble. Dry silk that may only weigh a pound suddenly becomes about five pounds when wet. My grand plan had been to wash, tilt the can to drain off soapy water, refill with hose water, and repeat until totally rinsed. However, just moving the silk in the water was like lifting boulders. Once started, however, I had no choice but to continue my ill-fated procedure. After a long time of tugging, pushing, and pounding on the silk lump in the soapy water, I started to tilt the can to let some of the water slosh out. I braced one foot on the can's bottom and held on to the can's lip with both hands as I tilted the container. The water moved to the edge. All seemed well. But then the "dye devils" arrived. Suddenly the flexible plastic started stretching. I pulled frantically in the opposite direction of the pouring water, but the can only elongated more. The balance of power shifted instantly and a heavy wet lump of silk slid over the lid and into the dirt. Over the tumbling can I came, landing on the silk in a rush of water. Since this experience, I have accepted that silk, no matter how expensive it is, can be machine washed.

Machine Washing Silk

Avoid any soap or detergent that contains alkalies. Even weak alkalies such as borax, ammonia, and phosphate of soda can deteriorate the fiber and diminish luster.[12]

Remember that when the silk moth is ready to emerge from its cocoon, it excretes an alkaline liquid to dissolve the silk filaments and create its escape hole. So take a clue from nature.

Neutral, non-alkaline dishwashing soaps, such as clear Ivory liquid, work well. Laundry detergents should be avoided as

most have alkali added for better cleaning power. Never use chlorine bleach on silk.

1. Set your machine on the delicate cycle. Gentle agitation is important as silk fiber is weaker when wet, but returns to its original strength when dry. Select a warm wash setting, but finish with a cool water rinse to minimize wrinkles. Many people subject their silks to higher temperatures and more vigorous washing than I do. Although the silk will survive, I feel it loses some of its "spirit" and luster.

2. Add a non-alkaline soap to the washer. If the fabric is very delicate or gauze like, encase it in a net washing bag, or a pillowcase tied at the open end.

3. Put the silk in the machine and let it run through the washing and rinsing cycles, but take it out before the final spin. Even though the silk will be quite wet, I prefer to remove it at this point. The spin cycle pressure sets the wrinkles, making them harder to remove later.

4. Either line dry the silk away from sunlight or iron it dry. I prefer to iron the fabric while wet or very damp, when the wrinkles are easy to remove. If you are unable to do so, keep the wet silk rolled up in a terry cloth towel and store it in the refrigerator.

Washing Rayon

Unless your rayon is very lightweight or sheer (follow silk washing instructions), rayon can be washed with the same procedure as cotton.

Ready-to-Dye Fabric

Instead of washing the fabric yourself, you can purchase already prepared fabric. Testfabrics is a company that sells all types of pre-scoured, desized fabrics that are ready to dye or paint. This service is especially helpful when you have a large quantity of fabric and would rather spend your time painting rather than preparing.

Chapter 2

THE COLORANTS

When you decide to dye or paint your own fabrics, you become part of an ancient tradition. The desire for colored cloth seems to have touched every century and country. Few of the early textiles have survived except as time-worn fragments. Even less remains to remind us of the early dyers—a street name in Florence, Italy (Corso de' Tintori), a reference in Chaucer's *The Canterbury Tales*, or a fading recipe book in some museum archive. Most of the time, we have to create a picture of our craft ancestors from a few good historical details and a lot of imagination.

From everything I've ever read about early dyers, I'm sure that they were very clever, observant, and inventive. They studied nature closely. They knew which berries stained, what leaf pounded into cloth would leave a chlorophyll imprint, and how that imprint could change colors if it were soaked in a certain stream, in sea water, or buried in wood ashes. Not only were their discoveries important to the coloring of cloth, but also to other early professions. As many natural dyes were medicines, the dyers' skill in identifying and cultivating plants was instrumental to the development of a more scientific approach to healing. Painters, too, owe their knowledge of many pigments to the dyers' early notebooks.

2-1 Cotton fabric painted with metallic fabric paints by Margaret Scott-Dobbins.

EARLY TEXTILE DYES

Because it often took years of experimentation to develop reliable recipes, early dyers were secretive and superstitious. Workers signed oaths and were threatened if they revealed any part of the process. Only a select few knew the recipes kept in carefully guarded notebooks. Outsiders were definitely unwelcome and discouraged from visiting the dye houses by rumors of terrifying apparitions that haunted the premises. Some cultures wouldn't allow "mean spirited" people to tend the dye pot in case their bad attitude might affect the dye's success. In Japan, sake is still offered to the indigo dye pot because it is believed to be a living substance. Many groups honored dye gods, such as Melkarth, the Phoenician god, whose sheep dog is supposed to have bitten a shellfish and discovered the color purple from his stained jaws.[1] Even modern day dyers agree that it doesn't hurt to have a dye goddess hovering around the studio, or to throw a good luck penny into the steamer pot before the fabric meets the heat.

As secretive and superstitious as the early dyers were, they probably didn't need to worry much about visitors. Only the most determined spy would have come near a dye house. As much as everyone admired their products, no one wanted to be their neighbors. The dyers' trade was considered a dirty, unclean occupation best exiled to the outskirts of town, next to the equally smelly tanners. You can't blame the townspeople when you think about some of the dye sources (insects, shellfish glands, algae) and extraction methods (boiling, salting, fermenting in urine).

The most difficult color to obtain was my favorite—purple. According to Gosta Sandberg,[2] the raw material for the purple dye was found in mollusks collected at the bottom of the Mediterranean sea. The piles of crushed shells (12,000 mollusks yield a small amount of dye) have helped historians pinpoint the locations of the old dye houses along the Mediterranean. Even some shellfish dyed textiles can be identified because of the slightly fishy smell clinging to their fibers. Perhaps it also explains why the aristocrats draped in their luxurious purple garments always wore copious amounts of perfume.

Strange that the revolution in dyeing methods in 1856 would be connected to the color of purple. Perhaps eighteen-year-old William Henry Perkin was thinking of purple's preciousness when his search for synthetic quinine produced only a dark precipitate.[3] Why else would he have dipped a piece of silk in it and discovered the first synthetic dye—mauve. Although his new coal tar derivative dye wasn't very colorfast, it was used immediately and stimulated more dye research. Scientists reasoned that if the difficult light purple could be produced in a laboratory, so could other colors. Returning to the natural dye sources one last time, they isolated and analyzed the coloring agents in each and began to reproduce them chemically. Soon other synthetic dyes followed in rapid succession: 1875 acid dyes, 1880 original azoic dyes, 1901 vat dyes, 1915 metal-complex dyes, 1923 dispersed dyes, and in 1956 reactive dyes.[4]

The dyer's life had become easier but totally transformed. Suddenly a lifetime of natural dyeing knowledge was obsolete. Unusual and rare plants no longer had a function and disappeared. Certain colors became lost to our eyes and can never be duplicated again. Not only had the source for the colors changed but also the connection. In natural dyeing the object from which the colorant is drawn usually has a beauty of its own, but with synthetic dyes and paints, the color "transcends the substances from which they are derived...beautiful colors thro artifice."[5]

FIBER REACTIVE DYES

Modern textile coloring agents are divided into two categories: dyes and paints. The main difference to remember is that dyes are transparent and can be made to dissolve in water and react with the fiber, either by chemically bonding or by coating. They become part of the fiber and cannot be felt on the fabric's surface. Fabric paints contain solid pigment particles, nonreactive and insoluble in water, that must adhere to the fabric. As they do not penetrate the fiber but lie on the fabric's surface, a very slight texture can be felt due to the binder, which glues them to the fabric. Many of the techniques in this book can be done with either colorant once you understand the different qualities each will give.

We will start first with dye. The dye I have chosen to use for most of the techniques in this book is the fiber reactive dye. It is my favorite because it adapts to many techniques, is very reliable and permanent, doesn't require toxic chemicals in its process, and is easy to use by everyone once the simple recipes are learned. Most of all, though, I trust this dye. The test of a good dye is what the product looks like years after it is dyed. I have colored everything from cloth, wood, and paper to straw with these dyes. Even after much use and exposure to light, I have still been pleased with the color years later. Although I do use other dyes for some projects and invite you to experiment with all the new ones on the market, I still return to fiber reactives for most of my work. It is simply the most dependable and versatile dye in my experience.

First developed in 1956 by ICI (Imperial Chemical Industries, Ltd.), fiber reactive dyes are derived from petrochemicals. Although a synthetic dye, they will not color synthetic fabric. The fibers they will dye are all natural: cotton, silk, viscose rayon, and linen. Wool can be dyed but requires special treatment. Only processes for cotton, silk, and viscose rayon will be covered in this book. The reactive dyes are very permanent as the fiber molecule chemically bonds (or reacts) with the dye molecule. Fiber reactive is the classification name, but the dyes may be sold under various brand names, such as Cibacron® F, Procion®, Dye House®. Although all fiber reactive brands work in a similar manner, they should not be intermixed as reactivity and process differences exist. The information in this book is for Procion® dyes, the MX and H series. If you are using another brand, read the manufacturer's instructions before beginning to check for differences. The techniques, however, will work with all brands. Before beginning any of the patterning processes in this book,

be sure to return to this chapter to review the technical information and recipes.

Procion® MX Series

The basic procedure for all fiber reactive dyes is to mix the colors, add an alkali (activator) that starts the chemical reaction, apply the dye, and later set the fabric to make the colors permanent. However, you do have a choice as to whether you want to use the MX series which reacts quickly or the slower reacting H series.

If you only want to stock one dye, the MX series would be a good choice as you can use it both *for immersion dyeing* (one-color dye bath) and *for direct application techniques* in this book (painting, stamping, spraying, etc). The dye comes in *powder form* with approximately *112 ready-mixed colors* from which to choose. The dye powder will last up to three years if stored in a dark, dry, cool environment, and is economical and easy to use.

The MX series is a *very reactive dye*, meaning that the minute it gets wet it begins to change chemically and bond with the water or cloth. For this reason, it isn't sold in liquid form like the H series. Once the dye powder has been mixed with water to make a dye solution, it will last three to four days if it is not activated by adding alkali. If refrigerated, it will last two to three weeks as the cold slows the dye's reaction with the water. Once the alkali activator has been added to the dye solution, either in the form of an activator mixture (part soda ash, part baking soda) or as pure baking soda (bicarbonate of soda) (see page 17), the *dye is good for only four hours.*

Because you want to be sure you get a full four hours of use, never add pure soda ash, which is a strong alkali, to activate your dye solutions. If you do, 10 percent of the dye will react with the water in your cup in approximately 10 minutes, with another 10 percent the next 10 minutes. In a short time, you could lose the dye's potency before it ever hits the fabric. If you need more than four hours to complete a very complex process, you may want to consider the H series, which won't exhaust as quickly. The fast reaction time of the MX series does, however, make it the perfect dye for last minute projects; its fast reaction time means that it also bonds with the fabric in a short time. You can paint your fabric, set the dyes, and have the fabric you want in several hours.

Procion® H Series

The H series dyes were developed specifically for direct application methods that were slower to execute, such as printing, stenciling, hand painting, and silk screening. Because they have a *slower reaction time* than the MX series, they remain more stable once mixed with water. Accordingly, they are sold not only in powder form, but also as a liquid for those who wish to avoid working with the powders. The H powders keep as long as the MX powders, and the liquid H dyes will keep one year without color loss if the bottle is tightly capped and stored in a cool, dark place. Once diluted with chemical water (see page 16) to make the dye solutions, the H series will *maintain color strength up to one month.* Even after the alkali has been added, it will still remain strong for one month as compared to the four hours for the MX series. The ability to keep a color usable for weeks makes them the perfect dyes for commissions or large printing projects where only a few yards can be completed in one day.

The H series also has several other differences. You will need to mix more colors yourself as *fewer ready-made colors* are available (approximately 18–22). The H series is less convenient to use for immersion dyeing than the MX series as it requires a higher processing temperature (175°F). Additionally, the H series dyes cannot be batch set (see page 18). Instead they *require heat for permanent fixation* (iron, clothes dryer, or steamer) with steam giving the most brilliant colors. And should you find yourself with leftover dye from both the MX and H series, resist mixing them together as they react at different rates and temperatures. However, the powdered H and the liquid H dyes can be combined.

Safety Precautions

Whatever series you decide to use, dyes are like other art materials and should be used correctly. Dyes are chemicals, so don't ignore the manufacturer's safety recommendations or procedure sequence. Fiber reactive dyes are some of the safest dyes available. According to the manufacturer, they are non-toxic, contain no known hazardous ingredients, and pose no confirmed health risks except for allergic reactions in sensitive individuals. However, whether I'm working with a household cleaning product or a dye, I always use the maximum amount of protection to minimize any possible health risks. When purchasing dyes, always ask for the manufacturer's instructions, which list safety precautions. If you want to know more about your dyes, you can request a MSDS (material safety data sheet) from your supplier.

• Purchase separate utensils for dyeing (pan, measuring spoons and cups, plastic bowls, etc.), and never mix them with your food preparation equipment. If possible, confine your dyeing to your studio, garage, spare room, basement, or outdoors. If you must work in the kitchen, clear and cover your counters, and be meticulous about cleaning up afterward. Do not eat, drink, or smoke while dyeing.

• Keep dyes, chemicals, and tools away from children and pets. Do not use dyes when you are pregnant as the health risks are currently unknown.

• Wear a dust mask or NIOSH-approved respirator with replaceable filters when mixing powdered dyes to avoid inhaling dye powders. If you wear contacts, always wear safety goggles so no powder attaches to the lenses. Use procedures that minimize dye contamination, such as turning off fans and air conditioners when measuring out dye powders. Replace lids on containers immediately. Mix your custom colors after the dye powders have been added to water and are liquids. Wipe up spilled powders or solutions immediately.

• Avoid skin contact with the dyes or auxiliary chemicals. Wear old clothes and kitchen rubber gloves when mixing dyes, rinsing dyed fabric, cleaning up spilled dye, or working in a method where the hands contact the dye solution.

Think about the technique you are doing and then use common sense. Your safety requirements can be quite different depending on the technique. Painting with thickened dyes may require only lightweight flexible surgical gloves. Sprayed dyes, however, become airborne and you will want to wear a respirator and goggles, as well as long sleeves and pants to keep the dye off your body.

RECIPES FOR DYEING WITH FIBER REACTIVE DYES

Fiber reactive dyes can be used like watercolors, very liquid and flowing, or thickened to create a painting paste. Either way, mixing the consistency you want is like following a recipe for baking a cake. Although the information below may seem like a lot of steps, it's because I have tried to explain how some of the ingredients work at the same time.[6] If you understand why an element is added, you will have a better chance of solving your own dyeing problems and re-creating interesting accidental effects. After you read and follow the procedure once, you will quickly see how the information condenses into a few easy-to-use recipes. In no time you'll have them memorized and can proceed to any chapter without a technical review.

Recipes for Watercolor Effects

A. Prepare the Chemical Water

In immersion dyeing, the fabric is submerged in a container filled with a one-color dye bath. As the fabric stays in the dye bath for anywhere from 20 to 60 minutes, the chemical action of the dye has plenty of time to react with the wet fiber. In direct application methods, however, the dyeing takes place on the surface of the fabric. It dries quickly, shortening the time the dye can bond with the fiber. To ensure that the proper dyeing conditions occur during direct application methods, several auxiliary chemicals are added to the water in which the dyes are mixed, hence the name "chemical water."

1. Urea pellets are made from an ammonia compound containing 46 percent nitrogen, and help to maintain moisture in the fabric so the dyes have longer to complete their reactions. They also aid in dissolving the dye particles when mixing dyes with the water. If you work in a very humid environment, the amount of urea can be reduced slightly. But never go below six tablespoons of urea per quart of water. Urea can be purchased from dye suppliers or a fertilizer store (ask for "tapioca" urea).

2. Sodium hexametaphosphate (Calgon, water softener, Metaphos) is added to regular tap water to neutralize any minerals (metallic ions) that could interfere with the dye's action.

> **THE RECIPE:** In 2 cups of hot tap water dissolve 10 Tbs. of urea. Add 2 cups cold water to make 1 quart of chemical water. If you have very hard water, add 1 tsp. of sodium hexametaphosphate (or Calgon, Metaphos, water softener) to the chemical water. Be sure the chemical water is cool before adding the dye.

B. Add Dye to the Chemical Water

Put on your face mask, goggles, and rubber gloves. Pour one cup of chemical water into a measuring cup. Then pour a small amount from the measuring cup into a plastic or glass container (plastic tumbler, glass jar). Remove lid from powdered dye, spoon out 2 tsp. (to achieve a medium shade), replace lid, and place powder on top of chemical water in the container. Stir until a smooth paste is formed. Add remaining water from the measuring cup into the container. You now have one cup of dye solution in a stock color (as it comes from the manufacturer).

> **THE RECIPE:** Add 2 tsp. powdered MX or H series fiber reactive dye to 1 cup chemical water.

If any powder has spilled on a surface, wipe it up with a wet paper towel. Once the powdered dye has dissolved and can no longer be inhaled, your mask and goggles can be removed. If you are using liquid H dyes instead of the powdered dyes, follow the manufacturer's recommendations for dilution proportions.

I usually mix up an assortment of stock colors in jars and then begin creating blends. When mixing custom colors, it helps to have some understanding of color theory. Many excellent reference books exist.[7] I recommend that you read and study as many as you can but stop immediately if you feel color paralysis set in. Remember that color is not only scientific, but a joyous, emotional component of our work. It is also a shifting, rather mystical and deceiving element. On a chart, a color has one face. But release it into your work and surround it with other colors, and it changes like a chameleon.

Once you've worked with colors a while, there can be no doubt that they have their own personalities. That's why I suggest that you spend time mixing and playing with each dye you purchase. I like to make 3" x 3" squares from the fabrics I use the most (the color will be different on cotton or silk). For each color, I paint a dark, medium, and light value square and make notes on the back. Then I cut the squares apart.

I find the individual squares most useful when I'm in the middle of painting and am trying to find the right color for the next section. By placing the squares directly onto the work, I can see immediately how the ambient colors will affect my choice. When I find the square that is nearest to the color I am seeking, I begin mixing the new color from the notes on the back.

As all colors dry lighter, I do one more test swatch. I paint my newly mixed color on a scrap piece of the fabric I'm using, dry it with a hair dryer, and then place the swatch on the work to be sure I have exactly what I want. Dyes cannot be erased. If the last color I add to a complex silk painting is wrong, my weeks of work are wasted. So I take the time to check each new addition before the brush touches my fabric.

Besides, even if I plan each color, the dye takes pleasure in surprising me. Unlike pigments, which are inert and predictable in mixtures, dyes can be quirky and lively. For instance, if I mix the MX turquoise and fuchsia together I will get the wonderful purple I'm expecting. However, when I brush the color onto the fabric, the turquoise often separates and rushes ahead of the mixture. If allowed to dry on its own, I will have a beautiful purple shape edged in turquoise where I expected just a solid purple color. I've also learned that turquoise may give the appearance of being aggressive, but it washes out more than other colors during rinsing; I always mix it stronger. Fuchsia on the other hand may be slow moving, but it penetrates and stains the fabric quickly and permanently. A little powder goes a long way.

Getting to know your dyes will imprint their characteristics in your color memory. If you don't take time to experiment, you'll never discover the beautiful gray a diluted black gives, or the rich watermelon a medium-value scarlet releases, or the mellow tans that are hidden in the rich browns.

C. Activate the Dye Solution with Alkali

Both the MX and H series require an alkali to start the chemical reaction between the fiber and dye molecules. Think of the alkali as a catalyst that gets the molecules moving about and forming the chemical links. The alkalis commonly used are soda ash (also known as sodium carbonate, washing soda, sal soda, and "fixer"), baking soda (bicarbonate of soda), or an activator mixture (a combination of the two). Do not purchase the washing soda (soda ash) sold in supermarkets as it has additives that will interfere with the dyeing process. Also replace your baking soda stock frequently as it needs to be fresh.

The dye may be activated with alkali in two ways. In method 1 the fabric is soaked beforehand in soda ash. When the dye is applied later, it connects with the activator already in the fabric. Do not use on silk. In method 2, either baking soda or the activator mixture is added directly to the container of dye solution and then applied to the fabric. With method 2, the MX dyes will last only four hours. You must also remember to add the alkali to every color before painting or the dyes will not begin the chemical reaction and will wash out during rinsing.

Method 1: Alkali Activator Added to Fabric

1. Pour 1 gallon of warm (95°F) tap water in a tub. Add 9 Tbs. of soda ash. Stir until particles are completely dissolved.

2. Soak the fabric for approximately 15 minutes in the solution, turning frequently. Wear rubber gloves as the soda ash can be irritating to the hands. The fabric does not need to be dry when added to the tub, but it should not be so wet as to dilute the alkali solution.

3. Wring out the fabric to remove excess solution, but do not rinse. The fabric may be dyed while wet, or dried and stored for future use. Cotton may be placed in a clothes dryer as it can withstand the combination of alkali and high temperatures. Other fabrics should be line dried or spread out to dry. If needed, the fabric may also be ironed to remove wrinkles that might cause uneven dye penetration in some techniques.

4. Save the soda ash solution as it can be reused. Cover the container to prevent evaporation and add more soda ash as the solution weakens through use. The process may also be done in the washing machine as long as no rinsing occurs.

THE RECIPE: Add 9 Tbs. of soda ash to 1 gallon of warm water (95°F). Soak fabric 15 minutes.

Method 2: Alkali Activator Added to Dye in Container

FOR COTTON AND RAYON: Add 1 tsp. activator mixture to 1 cup dye solution. The activator mixture is made by combining two alkalis— 4 parts baking soda and 1 part soda ash (or PRO Chem activator). For example: 4 teaspoons baking soda are added to 1 tsp. soda ash and stirred well. Then 1 tsp. of this mixture is added to each cup of dye solution.

As alkali is detrimental to silk, method 2 is used as it shortens the time the alkali contacts the fiber. Also a milder alkali, baking soda, is substituted for the activator mixture as an extra precaution. Although silk activated with baking soda can be batch set (24–48 hours), better results are obtained if the fabric is air dried and then heat set by ironing, clothes dryer, or steaming.

THE RECIPE: *Cotton and Rayon*: 1 tsp. of activator mixture to 1 cup of dye solution. *Silk*: 1 tsp. of baking soda to 1 cup of dye solution.

D. Complete the Technique

Once the dyes are prepared and activated with alkali, follow the technique instructions found in each chapter.

E. Set the Dyes in the Fabric

To make the colors permanent and colorfast, all fabrics dyed with fiber reactive dyes must be "set" with one of the following methods.

Batch Setting or "Batching"

Before the fabric dries, cover completely in a sheet of plastic and allow to dry as slowly as possible. If the fabric is damp, it can be sandwiched between two plastic sheets and rolled up to save space. If the fabric is very wet, however, it must be covered and left in place to dry. The fabric should remain moist for a minimum of 4 hours if you are rushed, but 24–48 is better. The room temperature must be 70°F or above during that time period. If your studio temperature drops too low at night, or if the fabric dries too quickly, the dyes will not set properly. Remember that batch setting is for MX dyes only. The H series requires heat setting.

Iron Setting

Slowly move a medium hot iron over a small section of the fabric for about three to five minutes. Iron temperatures vary, so although you want the hottest temperature appropriate to your fabric, beware of scorching. Try to keep all the fabric in that one area warm for the full amount of time. When one section is set, move to the next. Although this is a rather tedious activity, it doesn't require much concentration and can be done while enjoying your favorite television programs.

Clothes Dryer Setting

Fabrics (except silk) that are completely dry may also be set by tumbling for 45–60 minutes in a clothes dryer on the hottest setting. Commercial dryers are best as they reach higher temperatures. Avoid putting fabrics with resists (gutta, wax) into the dryer as some of the materials could melt and stick to the walls.

Steam Setting

Somehow steam setting has acquired a reputation of being too complex or too laborious. Yet steam setting is the only method where you can be sure that your fabric is reaching the proper temperature and moisture to set the dyes in a controlled environment. The effectiveness of other methods can vary depending on your equipment, your mood, the ambient moisture, room temperature, etc. Best of all, steaming yields the brightest colors with the least washout. If you work with wax processes, it can not only set the dyes but remove most of the wax at the same time. Steaming is also an efficient production method. You can let the painted fabric dry, store each piece to free up more studio space, and when you are ready, do one steaming and set many yards of fabric in an hour. And it's really not difficult once a basic system is set up.

Homemade Steamers

Although professional steamers are available, a very efficient and economical home steamer can be made from a large enamel canning pot with a wire bottle rack, which will hold the fabric.

Before placing the fabric in the steamer, it must be protected from condensation. The easiest method is to sandwich the fabric between sheets of blank newsprint (available as packing paper from moving companies) rolled into a tube and coiled into a loose spiral-shaped bundle. The newsprint protects the fabric from water spots and also absorbs melting wax. The bundle is secured with string or wrapped with masking tape and must be small enough to fit into the pot without touching the sides or the lid.

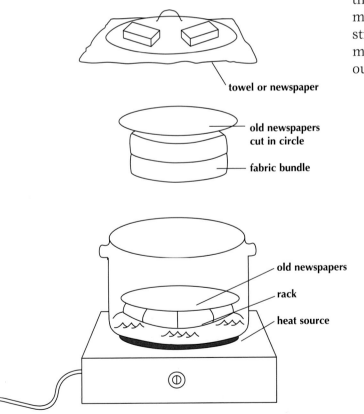

towel or newspaper

old newspapers cut in circle

fabric bundle

old newspapers

rack

heat source

Fig. 2-1 Canning Pot Steamer

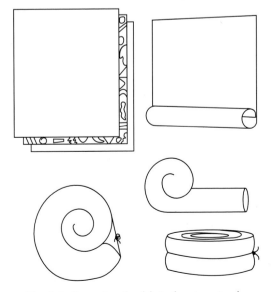

Fig. 2-2 Preparing the fabric for steaming by rolling in blank newsprint

Place the canning pot on the stove or an electric hot plate. Fill the pot with 1" to 2" of water; the depth depends on the elevation of the bottle rack. Place a layer of old newspapers cut in a circle on the rack to keep splashes from below from reaching the bottom of the fabric. Do not allow the newspaper to touch the sides of the pot. Turn on the heat, cover, and when steam rises, set the fabric bundle on the newspaper-covered rack. Place another layer of newspapers on top to catch any condensation dripping from above.

Next lay a folded towel or more newspaper over the opening of your pot. Let it extend over the edge of the pot to prevent steam from escaping. Weight the cover with a few bricks to help build pressure. Be sure the towel or newspaper does not extend too far over the edge of the pot or it may catch fire.

Begin timing. How long you steam will depend on the type of dye, fabric density, and the amount. MX dyes will fix in a shorter time (approximately 20 minutes) than the H series (approximately 45 minutes). A thinner fabric such as China silk will allow the steam to penetrate more quickly than a dense cotton fabric. And of course, if you have $1/2$ yard in the steamer versus three yards, it's obvious that the steaming times will differ. With experimentation, you will arrive at the right temperature and time for your equipment.

Remove the lid carefully to allow the steam to escape before reaching inside. Remove the fabric bundle and unroll. If it has steamed sufficiently, tiny wrinkles, or puckers, will appear at various points throughout the fabric's surface. If not, roll again and steam a bit longer. After steaming, wait at least 24 hours before rinsing.

If very wide fabric or many yards need to be steamed, the canning pot can easily be extended into a vertical steamer. Place a 10" wide, 5 to 6 foot long stove pipe or galvanized steel air conditioner duct pipe into the canning pot. Roll your fabric (sandwiched between paper) onto a cardboard fabric tube or chicken wire formed into a tube and secure with tape. Lower the tube into the pipe, and suspend it from some type of hanging device (bent hanger, dowel rod) so it doesn't touch

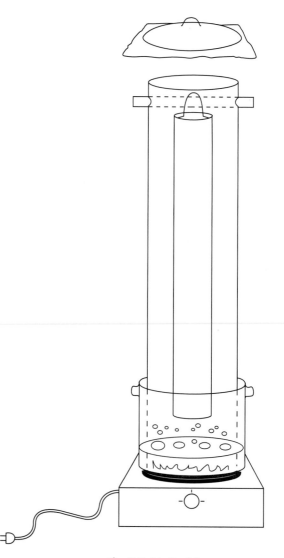

Fig. 2-3 Vertical Steamer

the water in the canning pot. Cover the top of the pipe with newspaper, put on the lid and steam. Be sure pipe is balanced and secured in the canning pot so it won't wobble or fall over when boiling begins. The pipe gets very hot during steaming, so do not allow children or pets close.

To me, pulling fabric from steam clouds is the perfect finale to the creative process. Like a potter who gives the clay piece to the kiln to be transformed, I like the idea of giving my finished fabric to the heat of a steaming pot. Even if the colors didn't become more brilliant, I would probably steam anyhow as the ritual attracts me. I enjoy listening for the pot to sing, throwing in my old lucky penny, watching steam rise on a cold day, smelling the hot fabric as it unrolls. But for you, the pleasure might be in the slow movement of a heavy iron sliding across color, or the tumbling sound of a dryer as you rush about doing other things, or the sight of glistening fabric marinating under plastic.

Try all four setting options. Find the method that fits your space, lifestyle, and natural working rhythms. A process is only hard if it gives no pleasure.

F. Rinse the Fabric

Fabrics dyed with fiber reactive dyes must be rinsed to remove auxiliary chemicals and excess dye that wasn't taken up by the fiber molecules. The fabric will be slightly lighter after rinsing, but will hold its color well in subsequent washings.

If you do not need the fabric immediately, it is preferable to allow the dye to age a minimum of 24 hours or up to a week before rinsing. When doing a lot of yardage, sort the pieces into color groups. To hand rinse, begin with cool water and keep the fabric moving. Remember to wear rubber gloves. Continue rinsing until water runs clear; then do a final wash with soap and warm water. If using a machine, fill it to the highest level with cool water, no soap, and add the fabric after agitation has begun. Wash on a short cycle, three to five minutes, then switch the dial to spin to drain off most of the colored water. Don't allow it to complete the spin cycle. Immediately reset the dial to a warm wash. After rinsing and spinning, stop the machine, open out the fabric, and remove any knots. If the fabric feels slimy, alkali is still present. Reset machine for a hot water wash with a mild detergent and let it complete this cycle. For silk use a mild dishwashing detergent such as Ivory, Palmolive, or Joy.

Look at the suds as the fabric washes. If they are colored, or if a clear glass dipped into the water shows the water is still colored, you may need extra rinsing. Temperature should not exceed 185°F for silk or the luster can be diminished; this is usually not a problem unless your water heater is set to a very high temperature. Cotton or rayon fabric can

be dried in the dryer, but line dry silk.

You will probably devise your own rinsing technique depending on your equipment. The important part is to keep the fabric moving so it doesn't contact other sections or allow one color to bleed into the next. If you have a lot of white or light colored areas in your design, you may want to use a special detergent called Synthrapol (2 tsp. per gallon hot water or 3 Tbs. per washer load). Besides its use as a scouring agent in preparing fabric, Synthrapol also removes the nonreacted dye from the fabric and suspends it so it doesn't deposit onto another area. Should you discover that a color has migrated into unwanted areas, wash the fabric again immediately. The longer the escaping color stays in the fabric, the more permanent the stain becomes.

RECIPES FOR THICKENED DYE EFFECT

For some techniques, the dye will need to be thickened somewhat to slow its movement through the fabric, or thickened a lot to form a paste consistency for certain painting or

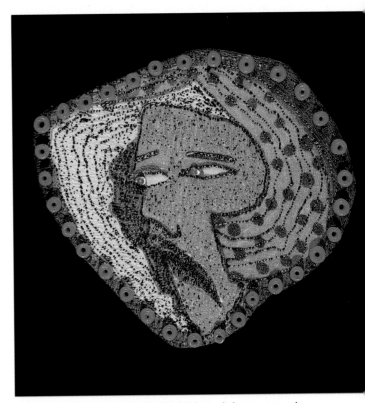

2–2 The face was painted with thickened dye paste and embellished with machine stitching. By Carolyn Dahl.

21

printing methods. The most common ingredient used to thicken dye is sodium alginate, which comes from a species of seaweed. It can be purchased separately, often called "thickener," or simply "alginate," or by various brand names. Or it can be purchased in combination with other ingredients as a "print paste mix," so named because it is most often used in printing processes. Either way, the dried sodium alginate powder (will keep approximately two years) swells when added to water making a gelatinous substance into which the dye can be suspended. Unlike starches or gums, sodium alginate thickeners do not chemically bond with the fabric's structure nor react with the fiber reactive dye. Thus the maximum conditions for dyeing are maintained because it doesn't interfere. The thickened paste is easily removed during the rinsing procedure.

Two types of sodium alginate are available. The first is known as a high viscosity, low solids content type of alginate (such as PRO Thick SH from PRO Chemical and Dye), which will yield a very thick paste with a small amount of alginate powder. It can be used on all fabrics and is the one you will use for the techniques in this book. If, however, you need a very fine line definition on a lightweight fabric such as China silk, then a second type (low viscosity, high solids) can be used (such as PRO Thick F). Follow the manufacturer's instructions for this second type as more will be needed to achieve the same paste thickness.

The thickener can be mixed to any degree of viscosity. I generally prefer to make a very thick paste from the ready-to-use mix (recipe 3) and thin it as needed for different techniques. The paste will keep for several months in the refrigerator if no dye activator has been added. Mark the jars "do not drink" and seal the lids with tape as an extra precaution.

Three recipes for thickening your dye solution with sodium alginate follow. Recipe 1 uses no additional chemicals. Recipe 2 includes Ludigol® (also known as resist salt), which will increase color yield when steam setting. Recipe 3 is a ready-to-use paste mix that produces a very thick mixture. The thickness or thinness of recipes 1 and 2 can be

changed by varying the amount of alginate used.

Recipe 1

Add $1^1/_4$ tsp. Metaphos (sodium hexametaphosphate, Calgon) to 1 quart chemical water and stir. Sprinkle 5 tsp. sodium alginate SH a little at a time on top of the water, and stir until particles are dissolved. Repeat this process until all of the alginate has been added. Stir for 5 to 10 minutes until the lumps disappear. Allow the solution to stand overnight. This paste uses no additional chemicals; however, it requires more time to become smooth.

Recipe 2

In 3 cups of hot tap water (120°–140°F) dissolve:

2 tsp. Metaphos (sodium hexametaphosphate, Calgon)

$1^1/_2$ tsp. Ludigol® (or PRO Chem® flakes)

$6^1/_2$ Tbs. urea

Add 8 tsp. sodium alginate SH a little at a time and stir as you go to dissolve the lumps. Add additional water to make 1 quart of thickened paste. I prefer to make the mix in a glass jar, which I can cap and shake vigorously. After mixing, let the paste set for at least 6 hours or overnight to achieve a smooth consistency.

Recipe 3

To make 1 cup of paste: Add $5^1/_2$ Tbs. of PRO Paste Mix SH (ready-to-use mix from PRO Chemical and Dye) to 1 cup room temperature tap water, adding and mixing a little at a time. Let the mixture set for 4–6 hours or overnight. When the thickened paste is ready, the dye can be added directly to the paste. Dissolve the powdered dye first in a little chemical water. Add approximately 2 tsp. powdered dye to 1 cup of paste. If adding liquid dye the amount can be judged visually. Once the color has been added to the thickened paste it is called dye paste.

When you are ready to activate the dye paste, dissolve 1 tsp. activator mixture in a small amount of chemical water and add to one cup of dye paste. For silk, use l tsp. baking soda per cup. To thin the dye paste, use chemical water mixed 7 tsp. urea (or 2 Tbs. plus l tsp.) per l cup tap water.

Once you have completed your project with the thickened dye paste, follow the instructions for heat setting and rinsing the fabric found on pages 18–21.

Disposal of Dyes

Do not pour your dyes onto the ground. They can reach underground water levels or wash into streams. Most dyes and auxiliary chemicals in the amounts studio dyers use can be disposed of in city sewer systems where they will undergo treatment. Flush the spent dye down the drain with lots of additional water to dilute the mixture. If you have a septic

system, contact your local water department for guidelines.

FABRIC PAINTS

The fabric paints we use are similar to fine artist's acrylic paints, which appeared in their water-based form around 1956. They consist of a pigment (the coloring agent) suspended in a polymer resin, which acts as the binder or glue. Acrylic resins are the most common, found in artist's acrylic paints, but other formulations are also used. Each resin gives the fabric a particular feel, which may be stiff, rubbery, or soft. After application of the paint, the water evaporates, leaving a strong film of color that is flexible, has good

2-3 In this work called ***Cosmic Cows*** fabric paint was used to paint over the dyed silk, to paint the wooden sticks, and as a glue for the jewels. By Carolyn Dahl.

2-4 ***Shaman's Coat*** by Margaret Scott-Dobbins. Createx metallic and pearlescent paint on leather, embellished with feathers, turquoise, and bones.

resistance to fading, and is insoluble once dry.

Several characteristics make using fabric paints different from using dyes. Dyes are transparent, joining their color with the color of the ground fabric to make a new color. With paints, however, you have several choices: transparent, semi-transparent, or opaque, when you want to completely cover the background color with a new color. (See 2-3, page 23.) Not only is a large range of colors available in these three types, but also in many specialty paints for achieving unusual effects: metallic, pearlescent (see 2-4, page 23), interference (reflects its complementary color), glitter, fluorescent, paint-on fibers and stars, and even glow in the dark. The paints may also be used as colored glue for attaching jewels or embellishments to the fabric.

Fabric paints are extremely easy to use. No special equipment, set up, health precautions (other than don't ingest the colors), or additional chemicals are required. You don't need to memorize recipes as the paints come

2-5 Detail of painted quilt batting.

ready-to-use and require no technical information to assure chemical reactions. The only heat setting required is ironing to increase wash fastness, and even that step has been eliminated by many manufacturers. The completed fabric doesn't even need to be rinsed, unless a paint odor remains. Another

2-6 In process shot of author painting cotton quilt batting with Createx fabric paints. Photos by Aileen Guggenheim.

24

2-7 *Space Age Ethnic* garment from "The Diamond Collection" fashion show. By Carolyn Dahl and Lisa Sharp. When my collaborator and I were chosen to participate in "The Diamond Collection" fashion show, I wanted to try something different. Because one of the sponsors was a batting company, Fairfield Processing Corporation, I decided to try the challenge of painting batting as if it were cloth. Instead of sandwiching it between two pieces of fabric, however, I wanted to use it as the outer fabric. When the Cotton Classic batting absorbed the Createx fabric paint, I was happy to discover that it became very felt-like, almost like handmade paper. Once it was quilted onto a background fabric, it was durable enough to survive a year of traveling to fashion shows around the country. Photo courtesy of Fairfield Processing Corporation. Photograph by Brad Stanton.

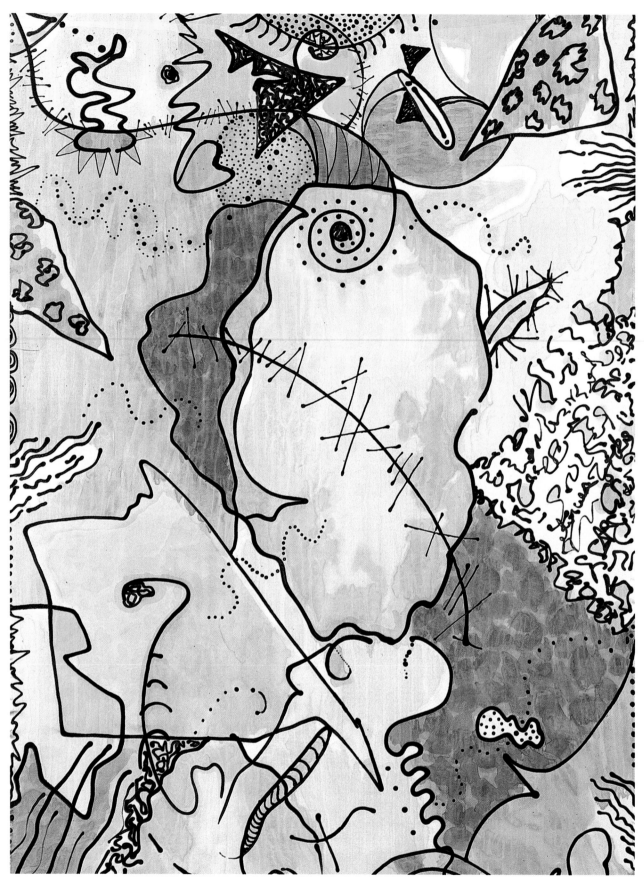

2-8 Detail of silkwork by Carolyn Dahl showing how fabric paint can be used thick or thin.

2-9 Granulation technique on manipulated silk.

advantage is that they will work on almost any fiber or blend as long as it is free of surface treatments—even cotton quilt batting. (See 2-5 – 2-7, pages 24–25.) It's great to be able to grab an old fabric whose content you've long ago forgotten and to start painting without any worry.

Every technique from fine lines and precise edges to wet watercolor washes to printing techniques can be created with the same jar of paint. (See 2-8, left.) If you like working in very wet washes, however, beware of diluting the paint too much and reducing its adhesive properties. It is best to purchase the manufacturer's "extender" which will allow you to dilute the color without breaking down the binder as plain water would. Also remember that if you like to work with thicker applications, the paint's binder will tend to stiffen the fabric slightly and have a plastic feel if used too heavily.

Although fabric paints have good fade resistance to ultraviolet light because the pigments are not chemically reactive like dyes, the colors are not as resistant to abrasion. After repeated machine washings, the agitation may break down the paint's binder that holds the color to the surface, and little by little the pigment rinses away lessening the vitality of the color. Of course, this is no prob-

lem if you're doing a wall piece that is seldom laundered. But if you use fabric paints on wearables, always turn the garment inside out and wash by hand or on a very gentle cycle to prevent this color loss.

When purchasing fabric paints, it is best to use those offered by textile dye suppliers or to stick with name brands. The characteristics of fabric paints vary with the manufacturer. You want a quality paint that has a high concentration of light resistant pigments and a pure binder with no added impurities to affect permanent adhesion. If a particular name brand is listed in the technique instructions, it means that I have obtained the best results with that product. It does not mean that others won't work. Any water-based fabric paint may be substituted, but the final effect could be slightly different.

Fabric paint may be called different names depending on the supplier: textile pigments, textile paints, fabric colors, fabric inks, and airbrush inks (thin, filtered, concentrated pigment). The products may all be pigments suspended in a synthetic binder, but vary in concentration, quality, viscosity, and additives. It is a good idea not to intermix brands as the chemical formulations may vary. Be sure, however, that the products are designated for fabric or the binder will not give a soft hand to your cloth.

You can also purchase the pigments separately and add them to the proper binder (also called medium) for your projects. For instance, if one day you're stamping on black fabric, you add your pigment to the opaque medium so the paint will cover the dark background. However, the next day you may want a transparent, sprayed color, so you add the same pigment to a thin airbrush medium, etc. This method reduces the different types of fabric paint you need to purchase and store. It also allows you to control the concentration of pigment particles on your fabric. Interesting granulation effects can be achieved by variations in the pigment-to-binder ratio. (See 2-9, above.)

Chapter 3

BLACK & WHITE TRANSFORMATIONS

$\mathcal{M}$y white cat doesn't know what a dangerous life he leads. As he passes through my studio, brushing against dye pots, I watch his smooth white surface. Lucky for him, he never stands still for long or sleeps too soundly near me. So far, he's a normal colored cat, but I keep dreaming about his other eight lives. Surely one of them could be pink.

Moonstone is not the only animal whose surface I have wanted to color. My idea for this process came from zebras. Watching their shifting black-and-white patterns at the zoo one day, I mentally began to color in the white stripes. I suddenly realized they had given me a good idea for transforming commercial fabric. I went right from the zoo to a nearby fabric store and purchased a yard of every black-and-white print they had. I even found a zebra design in cotton flannelette. The soft nap had an uncanny resemblance to zebra skin. Once home, I splashed, poured, sprayed, and painted dye on the fabrics. After drying, the black-and-white print had become multicolored. The black parts of the pattern had absorbed the dyes, but the once white areas were filled with bright colors. (See 3-2, right.)

BEGINNER'S PATTERNS

Whether I had applied the colors carefully or haphazardly, all the results were usable. The black pattern held the design together no matter what I did

3-1 The commercial market provides us with an endless array of black-and-white prints. Even if the same painting techniques were used over and over, each piece of fabric would look unique because of the pattern variety.

3-2 Placing the unpainted fabric next to the painted version shows the transformation process. The structured, commercial pattern is softened by the hand-painted colors.

in the white areas. Thus transforming black-and-white prints is an excellent technique for beginners as it gives you the confidence to combine colors, try various application methods, and get to know your dyes and paints. You simply cannot fail. And you never waste any fabric while learning.

Although black-and-white prints give the best and most dramatic results, other combinations can also be used such as red and white or blue and white. The only difference is that black absorbs other colors without changing its own color; whereas a red or blue will combine with the applied color to form a new one. For instance, if you are painting blue into the white area of a red-and-white fabric, the blue could bleed beyond the white and into the red, creating a purple or dark-ened edge. Not that this would be bad. Some wonderful, unusual, and surprising shades

can result depending on how deeply the hand-painted color is able to penetrate the commercially printed color.

When purchasing fabrics to transform, look for prints in which the white areas domi-nate. The more white space the fabric has, the more area for you to color. Prepare your fabric as usual, and use either dyes (thin or slightly thickened) or fabric paints, depending on the fiber content of your fabric. Remember you can't fail. The learning will take place while you do the process, so don't think about it. If you need a few suggestions to get you going, follow the methods below and then invent your own.

Coloring Book

Almost every child grows up with a coloring book. Whether you were one of those who stayed within the lines or transgressed freely with your crayons, we all enjoyed adding color to white images. Many black-and-white prints resemble coloring book pages and can be painted in a similar manner. Look for fabrics with large scale designs or recognizable subject matter such as flowers, animals, geometric forms, or figures. You don't want the color to bleed from one shape to the next, so here are a few helpful suggestions (see 3-3).

• Work on dry fabric taped at points to

newsprint or newspaper. Paper absorbs the colorant and lessens bleeding. Plastic keeps the fabric wet longer and promotes color blending.

• Use a moderately stiff brush and don't paint all the way to the edge of your shape. Allow a small margin where the color can bleed. If a white edge remains later, you can touch it up with more color.

• Don't overload your brush with color on the first application. However with dye, you must saturate the fabric enough for

3-3 The fabric in the center panel with its cats and flowers is a good example of a coloring book fabric. The background polka dot print was spray dyed using a plastic grid as a stencil.

the chemical reaction to occur. If you lift a corner of the fabric and do not see any dye spots on the back side, you may need to paint the shape again.

• If the dye moves too quickly, stop it by blotting with a paper towel. Or you can use a dry paint brush and stroke the color backwards — from the edge of the shape toward the center.

• Thickening the dye or using undiluted fabric paints may be necessary to color in small shapes or precise details.

Color Bands

Painting bands of color across a black-and-white fabric seems almost too easy, but it's the best method for establishing a directional movement to your colors. If you apply the colors in horizontal or curving lines, the effect will be a peaceful, gentle color flow. Whereas, vertical, diagonal, or zigzag bands create an energetic active color flow. The effect will depend on how much the black pattern shapes interrupt the color bands. If the print has large open areas of white, the bands will be more visible and the directional pull stronger. If the design is very dense, with a small proportion of white, the black part of the pattern will obscure most of the directional flow. Try a variety of lines: vertical, horizontal, diagonal, curved, broken, thin, thick, bleeding, or well-defined.

Atmospheric Color

Atmospheric effects are created when all the colors bleed together into a smoothly blended surface. The secret to making colors blend is lots of moisture in both your fabric and your colorant. One method is to dip your fabric in water, wring out the excess, place the fabric on plastic, and apply the color while the fabric is still very wet. Another approach is to spray the water onto the fabric. Because you want your colorant to spread, do not add any thickener to your dyes and dilute fabric paints to a fairly thin consistency. Remember, though, that your fabric is already saturated with water, which will lessen the intensity of

your colors and cause them to dry lighter. Limit your color palette to three to five colors applied to different sections of your fabric. Allow them to blend and form additional colors. If too many colors are used, the results may be muddy and lifeless.

Linear Bleed

Find fabrics that have lots of freely drawn black lines on an open white background. Everything about the fabric print should feel spontaneous and uncomplicated, like oversized scribbling. Put yourself into the same relaxed state of mind. Draw a few lines in the air to loosen your shoulder before beginning. Then load your brush with color and follow a line on the fabric. Try to mimic the gesture as you paint the inside curve of one, the outside of another, over the center of a third causing color to bleed on each side, or fill in an open circle until a color blush forms around its rim. Circle a dot, or spatter a broad area. Watch the colors spread and grow progressively lighter.

3-4 The energy of the black lines in this print has been maintained by painting over the lines and letting the dye bleed outward in a loose calligraphic style. The same linear bleed method was used on the red-and-white background fabric piece. Notice how the blue bled into the red around the shape causing a darkened rim of color.

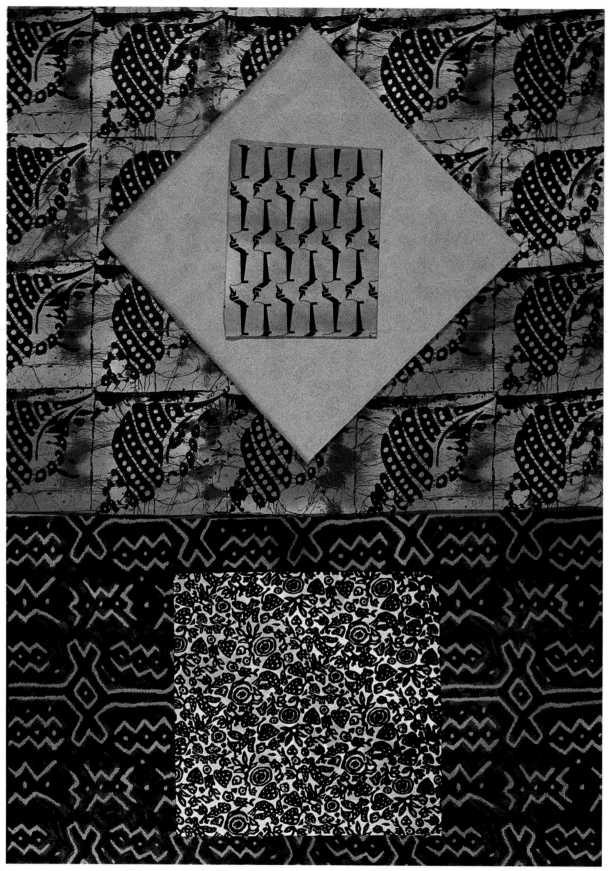

3-5 An assortment of black-and-white prints dyed with color bands, random blotches, and atmospheric blending.

Do leave a lot of pristine white in the background to provide a contrast to your energetic color lines. If you need inspiration, study pictures of Oriental calligraphy or Joan Miro's paintings. Be childlike and have fun with this process. (See 3-4, page 31.)

Color Blotches

Choose an assortment of colors that blend well when they bleed together. For example, if you mix five or six different shades of reds and blues and apply them in big circular shapes (or blotches), they will create attractive purples where their edges meet. Start with dry fabric and leave just enough space between shapes for the colors to bleed and connect. You can scatter the blotches across the fabric, line them up, vary sizes, or match them to some shape in the black-and-white pattern. Experiment with different tools such as a fat bristle brush, a natural sponge, a rag, or a foam applicator which will give a squarer shape when squashed onto the fabric.

Selective Focus

Sometimes in a black-and-white print, an intriguing shape will be hidden in the overall pattern. Often it only needs color emphasis to attract our attention (see 3-6, right). An interesting exercise is to select one pattern and do four different colorings, accenting a different shape each time. For instance, if I divide a yard of floral print fabric into fourths, I could focus my highlight color on the dominant shape, a rose, in the first piece and use subdued colors on all other shapes. For the second, I might select to highlight only the basket, in the third the leaves, and in the fourth the background textures. When all four

fabrics are sewn together again, I would have one pattern with four variations. The exercise forces us to notice the beauty in the secondary and background shapes. It's still the same black-and-white print, but when the dominant motif is determined by color placement, the fabric becomes new to our eyes.

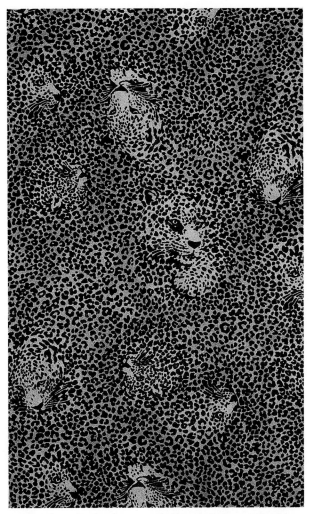

3-6 In the selective focus method, certain images in the print are emphasized through color. A light blue placed near the leopard's head makes the face stand out from the blotch-dyed background.

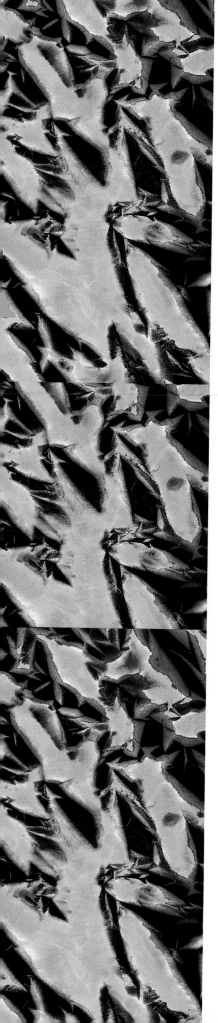

Chapter 4

BLENDED COLOR PATTERNS

Water is the vehicle that transports color across the fabric and into the fibers. So in a sense, whenever we paint, we paint with colored water. However, if little or no thickener has been added, and large amounts of color are applied to the fabric in a loose, juicy style, it's called color washing. The results depend on the fabric, the surface material under the fabric, the colorant type, and the position of the fabric. Although wonderful sections are created, don't think of color-washed fabric as a finished product. Consider it a beautiful base fabric to cut apart, embellish with stitching, enhance with beads, or combine with other surface design techniques in this book.

COLOR WASHES

The easiest color wash to execute is to lay the fabric flat on a plastic sheet and pour or paint on the colors. If nothing blocks or directs its progress, the colors will spread quickly through the fabric, leaving a softly blended pattern behind. The artist has little control over the results except for color placement. Instead one sits back and watches for the beautiful accidents to occur.

If, however, less blending and more area definition are wanted, an obstacle, or resist, is placed in the colorant's path. The resist can either slow or direct the colorant's flow, or totally stop or repel it. In this process,

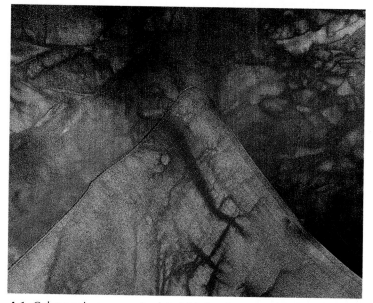

4-1 Color washes on manipulated fabric often resemble landscapes as they imitate sky, rock, and vegetation patterns.

34

4-2 Color washes on gauze-like fabrics can create interesting color overlays. In **Shaping the Water**, dyed silk organza and paper were combined with photocopied turtle images to create an underwater environment. By Carolyn Dahl.

4-3 Never discard any section of color-washed fabric. Although a color may look uninteresting after dyeing, once cut and pieced together with others, it gains a new vitality. Detail of ***Vault of Kept Promises*** by Melody Johnson.

4-4 The color-wash technique requires large areas of fabric to achieve its effect, so always dye at least two to three yards. ***Hot Fun*** by Melody Johnson.

the resist is a simple manipulation of the fabric. By wrinkling, folding, pleating, or scrunching the fabric, a three-dimensional resist consisting of hills and valleys is created. Now the color cannot flow smoothly and quickly, but must climb hills, get caught in the creases, or be directed along a fold line. All of this action distributes the color load unevenly as it dries, thereby creating different patterns on the fabric.

Procedure: Color Washes on Manipulated Fabric

1. Lay out 2–3 yds. of washed, wet or dry fabric (natural fibers), on a plastic sheet. Manipulate areas of the fabric into hills, valleys, folds, pleats, wrinkles, scrunched areas, etc.

2. Mix and activate fiber reactive dyes (see page 16). Now the fun begins. Pour some dye into a valley and watch it crawl slowly up the hill. Drip one color on top of another. Throw a little noniodized table salt into some wet colors for a speckled effect. Use a small paintbrush to apply dye onto a folded edge or inside a scrunched area. Spatter fine dots across an area by raking your finger over a toothbrush loaded with dye. Spray a slow moving color with plain chemical water to make it bleed further and become lighter. Be spontaneous, but don't overly saturate the fabric. Leave some white areas for a second application.

3. Wait 5 to 15 minutes so the fabric can absorb some of the dye and to see what patterns are developing. Now look for areas you like. Avoid adding liquid to these or even nearby areas. If a large pool of dye won't flow in a certain direction, lift the plastic sheet under the fabric to create a slight incline. Pushing it around with your hand (in a rubber glove) also works.

   Now add more dye only to those areas that need it. Work until you're almost satisfied. I say almost because the dye will continue to crawl as long as the fabric is wet, so more color blending will occur. If liquid threatens to obliterate a favorite

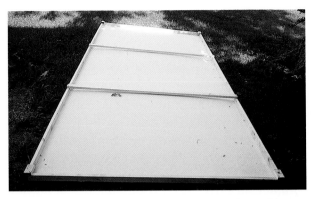

COLOR WASHES ON STRETCHED FABRIC

4-5 The 100 percent cotton (mercerized, bleached sheeting from Testfabrics) is stapled to a wooden frame. The photo shows the backside of the frame constructed out of l" x 2" lumber. Purchased wood, canvas stretcher bars and push pins can be used if your fabric size is 3' or less. The design is sketched lightly with a pencil on the front side of the taut fabric.

4-6 Using fiber reactive dyes, the design is painted and the cloth left on the frame two to seven days to set the dyes before washing. If some of the shapes need redefining, Caryl stretches the fabric again and outlines areas with fabric marker pens. The design is then cut into strips and alternated with a three-dimensional constructed tuck as they are sewn back together.

4-7 The finished quilt, **_Reflection #24_** by Caryl Bryer Fallert.

4-8 The dyer always hopes for those special sections where one color tugs and pulls on another leaving behind a colored shadow of the struggle.

spot, blot up the excess moisture with a paper towel. If it needs to be stopped quickly, use a hair dryer. Be careful, though, not to get the dryer too close, or the color could be blown into unwanted areas.

4. Do not move the fabric. To retain the pattern, it must remain in its manipulated, dimensional form until it is completely dry. Then spread out the fabric and enjoy the surprises that are hidden in the folds. Heat set and rinse according to dye directions.

If the fabric is stretched over a wooden frame and does not contact another surface, even more control can be exercised over the evolving shapes and colored areas. Although you are still washing on color with a loose, wet style, you now plan where you want the color washes instead of allowing the dye to dictate the pattern. Large simple images, well spaced, can be painted and will retain their shapes without too much bleeding. Caryl Bryer Fallert uses this method in her **Reflections** quilt series. (See 4-5 – 4-7, on page 37.)

SPRAY DYEING

Air surrounds us everyday. We cut through it as we walk and pull it in and out of our bodies every second. Yet it is only when we suddenly catch its dancing dust in a beam of sunlight do we believe it exists. By painting with a sprayer, however, we can reveal its invisible presence whenever we want. When dye or paint is propelled through a nozzle, it mingles with the air, dropping onto the fabric as tiny dots, much like fallen air bubbles. The artist never touches the fabric with hand or brush. This colored bubble texture is what gives sprayed fabric its distinctive beauty. One always feels the dyed air in the process.

Simply spraying many different colors and letting them blend optically on a flat fabric can produce beautiful misty, atmospheric effects. Or the fabric can be manipulated into folds, pleats, or other dimensional forms. When sprayed, only the top surface receives the color, causing free-form abstract shapes when the fabric is unfolded.

If you want more control, however, over

"Wherever you go today, tomorrow, or the rest of your life... You are part of someone's visual landscape... Why not make it beautiful?"
—C. Dahl, *"Wearable Art"* lecture

4-9 *Blue Norther Coat* by Carolyn Dahl and Lisa Sharp. Spray-dyed corduroy and velvet embellished with stitchery, appliqué, beading, and hand-dyed lace and yarn. Photograph by Michael McCormick.

the color development and shape placement, stencils can be used to develop more definite patterns. A stencil can be anything that blocks the dye or paint from reaching the fabric while preserving the color underneath. Even prehistoric people knew the simple principle of a stencil. In the cave paintings of Lascaux (France), some early artist placed a hand on the wall and sprayed color around it. Generations later, we still ponder this simple hand shape and wonder what tool served as a primitive sprayer; perhaps it was a hollow bone or cane.[1]

Stencils can be as simple as your hand, or as complex as an intricate Japanese stencil cut from paper impregnated with persimmon juice and smoke. Many objects from our everyday lives such as stick-on labels, doilies, plastic templates, feathers, masking tape, gutter screen, leaves, etc. work well as stencils. So experiment.

In the following procedure, torn newspapers are used as stencils with fiber reactive dye as the colorant. Fabric paint or airbrush ink may be substituted if it has been diluted to a spraying consistency. The basic process is simple as stencils are placed on the fabric and a color sprayed into the uncovered fabric areas. The stencils are then moved to a new position and a second color sprayed on. The process is repeated and new stencils are added until you're satisfied with the color overlays and pattern density.

Procedure: Spray Dyeing with Newspaper Stencils

As sprayed dye is easily inhaled, always wear a protective mask or respirator. Avoid contact with the spray by wearing rubber gloves and long sleeves. Work outside on a calm day or in a garage. Cover nearby objects as dye spray can drift. Review technical information for fiber reactive dyes before beginning.

1. Lay the washed, dried, and ironed fabric onto a plastic sheet or newspapers. Smooth out wrinkles and weight the corners well (bricks) if working outside.

2. Tear or cut newspaper into shapes—geometric forms such as triangles, circles, and

rectangles; amorphous and irregular forms; stripes, whatever—and arrange them on the fabric. Place weights (pennies, small tiles) on these shapes so your sprayer force doesn't lift them.

3. Pour dye (or diluted fabric paint or airbrush inks) into spray bottles. Plant sprayers and hair spray pump bottles will give an irregular spray pattern and some interesting drips. If you want a smoother looking spray, Preval® sprayers work well. Found at auto or paint supply stores, they have a glass bottle on the bottom with a screw-on canister of propellant (the power unit) on top (Fig. 4-1). Of course, an airbrush can also be used if you have one.

Fig. 4-1

4. Add dye activator to all spray bottles if using fiber reactive dyes, and if your fabric has not been presoaked in soda ash. Dissolve activator first in a small amount of water to prevent granules from clogging the nozzle.

5. Lightly mist the open areas of the fabric with the first color, for example pink. Avoid spraying at an angle or you may shoot spray under the edge of the stencils. You want distinct dots of color, not solid color, so don't over saturate the fabric (Fig. 4-2).

6. Allow the fabric to absorb the first color before moving the stencils, or the color will bleed into the shape. After approximately 3 to 10 minutes (depending on your fabric and saturation), remove the weights and reposition the newspaper stencils. Lower some stencils to reveal a white edge, or remove some completely. Cut holes or tear sections out of a few stencils and reposition on the fabric. Save areas of the first color (pink) by covering with new torn or cut newspaper shapes (Fig. 4-3).

7. Lightly spray on the second color, say

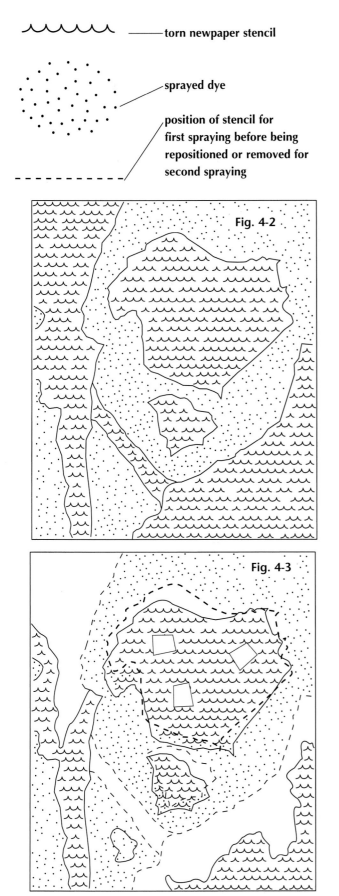

—— torn newspaper stencil

—— sprayed dye

position of stencil for first spraying before being repositioned or removed for second spraying

Fig. 4-2

Fig. 4-3

turquoise. Wherever the turquoise dye lands on pink areas, the two will combine into purple. When the turquoise falls on a newly-exposed white area, that section will become turquoise. Pink areas covered by stencils will remain pink. (See 4-10, below.)

8. Repeat this process. I usually find I can spray about five different colors before the dots disappear and muddy areas begin to develop. Additional colors may be used as accents and sprayed onto selected shapes. If the newspaper stencils become too wet at any time, replace them or they will not block the dye. Don't worry if you can't tear the exact shape again. A little edge variation adds depth and dimension to the shape.

9. Leave the last stencils in place until the fabric is fairly dry before removing. Allow the fabric to dry completely before heat setting. I do not recommend batch setting with this procedure as keeping the fabric moist could cause shape edges to bleed and become less definite.

4-10 A spray-dyed fabric in progress. Newspaper shapes and color overlays are starting to develop. Large areas of white remain to receive new colors.

4-11 Melody Johnson arranged her fabric into gentle folds before spraying, leaving lots of white for a snow-covered mountain effect in her **Hollyhocks** quilt. 37½" x 56".

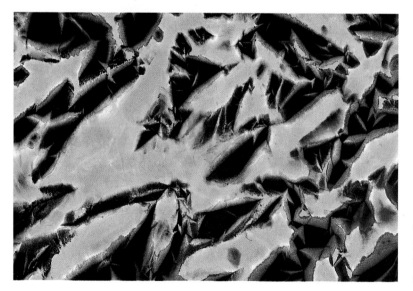

4-12 Scrunching and folding the fabric before spraying produces free-form shapes as only the top surface of the fabric receives color.

4-13 Puzzle pieces were used as stencils for this spray-dyed silk dress.
By Carolyn Dahl.

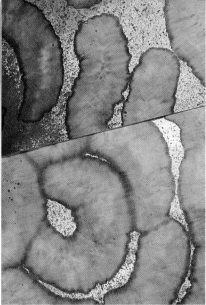

4-14 A new color was painted over a
freshly sprayed cotton fabric, causing the
spots to bleed and blend.

NATURE'S PATTERNS

Once I had a job with regular hours, interacting with other people, sitting behind a desk, reporting to a manager who reported to another manager. I didn't mind the work, but I constantly missed the sky. Sitting under fluorescent lights all day made me realize what a privilege it is to be an artist working for myself. To have the freedom to step outside any time of the day and to even work outdoors are reasons enough to have spent my life in the arts.

RAIN PATTERNING

Because fabric that hasn't been set is very susceptible to water spotting, especially silk, I often take advantage of nature's help by keeping fabrics ready for the rain. When a sprinkle arrives, I grab the fabric and rush outside. If there is no lightning, I enjoy standing by the fabric watching the drops move the dye around. Persuading the rain to stop at just the right point in my fabric design, however, has never been easy. So sometimes one has to start with a sunny day and make one's own rain.

When I saw Cheri Ruzich's hand-painted fabrics, they reminded me of my rain patterns. Surrounded by California orchards, she spreads out 25–50 yards of cloth over her 60 by 40 foot yard, squirts on fabric inks, and uses her garden hose to create her rain.

The images of a sky filled studio and a landscape covered in colored cloth were so appealing, I asked Cheri to share her technique for making her water-dappled fabric.

5-1 Rain patterned fabric by Cheri Ruzich. Photo by Margaret Mitchell.

Materials

Versatex airbrush ink in an assortment of colors, except white.

FABRIC: Cheri uses white 100% cotton print cloth (#400) from Testfabrics, but you may substitute any light colored fabric (natural or synthetic), as long as it doesn't have any surface treatments.

SQUIRT BOTTLES: Squirt bottles from Dharma Trading Company work well as they have very narrow spouts with caps to prevent the ink from drying, and are made of soft, easy-to-squeeze plastic.

FABRIC ANCHORS: Anything that secures the four corners of the fabric can serve as an anchor (stakes, bricks). Cheri recommends 9-gauge fence ties, which are thin wire rods for attaching cyclone fence material to the poles. She pushes the ties into the ground, one at each corner of the fabric, and attaches the cloth with clothespins.

PLASTIC DROP CLOTH: Laying your fabric directly on your lawn works best. Air is able to flow under the fabric, and excess water can drain away. The lawn will not be harmed or discolored if hosed off well after painting.

If you must paint on a paved driveway or patio, a plastic drop cloth should be used. Otherwise, the fabric will stick to the surface when it is dry and may be damaged. Also, the inks will stain cement permanently. The effect will be a little different when the fabric lays on plastic as the colors tend to puddle more.

GARDEN HOSE WITH FINE SPRAY NOZZLE: A nozzle with a handle is the easiest to control.

Procedure: Rain Patterning

1. Pick a sunny spot in your yard and a day when no rain is predicted. Try to begin work in the morning or early afternoon to ensure that your fabric will be dry by evening.

2. Wash 5 to 10 yards of fabric cut into desired lengths. After the spin cycle, remove the fabric from the machine and place it in a plastic bag to retain moisture.

3. Dilute the Versatex airbrush inks using a 3 to 7 ratio (3 parts of Versatex ink to 7 parts of water). Pour the diluted inks into squirt bottles and mix well by shaking at least ten times.

4. Remove one length of washed fabric from the plastic bag. Spread it out on the lawn and secure its four corners. Only one length will be painted at a time. If all the pieces were exposed to the sun at once, most of the fabric would be too dry for the inks to blend well.

5. Have all the squirt bottles nearby so you can switch colors quickly. Pick up one of the bottles and begin squirting color onto the fabric. The position of the squirt bottle will influence how the ink falls and the effect it creates. If you hold the bottle spout straight up, little droplets will result. If you point the spout toward the fabric, the ink will come out in a steady stream, which makes good lines. Finally, holding the bottle horizontally will give large droplets and allow more control over your pattern placement.

5-2 Airbrush ink is squirted onto the moist fabric and misted with a garden hose to blend the colors.

5-3 Cheri Ruzich's outdoor studio filled with colored cloth drying in the sun. Photo by Margaret Mitchell.

6. After the squirted design is on the fabric, it's time for the rain. Aim the garden hose away from your fabric at first and adjust the nozzle until a fine, even spray is produced. Then pivot toward the fabric and mist it lightly one or two times. Do not over saturate the fabric, or the colors will run off or blend into muddy puddles.

Should you find at this point that you don't like your rain pattern, or the neighbor's dog has just added its footprints, you can remove the ink by washing the fabric. Do it soon, however, as the longer the ink stays on the fabric, the harder it will be to remove.

Set your machine for a regular warm wash cycle, at the highest water level, and place the fabric in the machine after agitation has begun. Most of the color should disappear. Some color shadows may remain, but these can easily be painted over.

7. Those fabrics you intend to keep should be allowed to dry undisturbed in direct sunlight. If your fabrics are still wet when evening comes, slide them into your garage or to some other protected area.

8. When the fabrics are dry, heat set them with an iron set at cotton, or the highest temperature your fabric can bear. Go over each square foot of fabric for 20–30 seconds (in a well ventilated room). An easier method is to use a commercial dryer at a laundromat. Most home dryers will not reach the 250° temperature necessary to set the inks. There is no need to separate the fabrics by color, but do leave enough space in the dryer so they can tumble freely. Dry for 25 minutes at the hottest setting.

To remove excess ink and soften the cloth, machine wash the fabrics on a gentle, short cycle with regular laundry detergent.

After a day in the sun making rain patterned fabric, one thing becomes very clear. When you work outside, you never work alone. Bumblebees circle your head and check out your colors. Ants march across your fabric when the grass floods and ladybugs must be coaxed out of the drying paint.

46

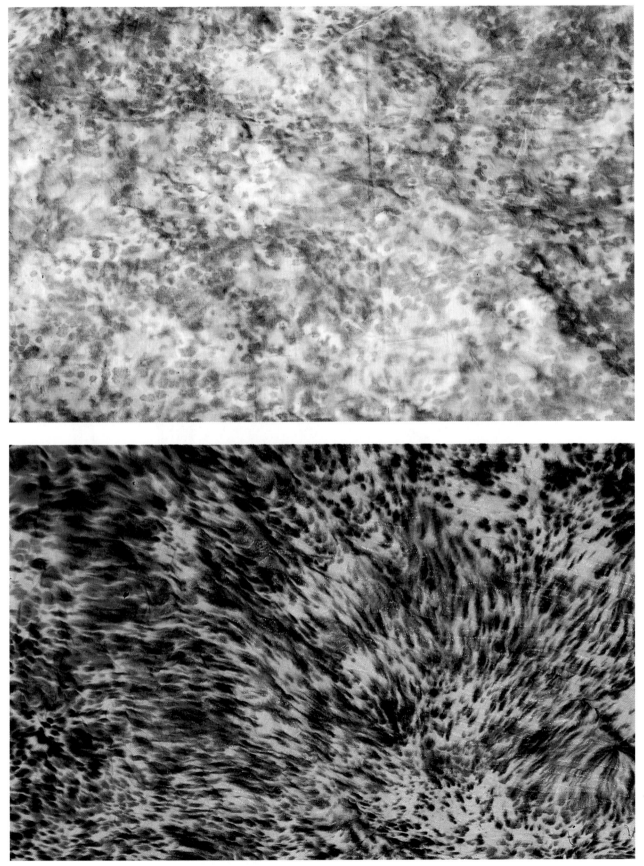

5-4 & 5-5 Rain patterned fabrics by Cheri Ruzich.

LEAF PRINTING

Knowing a leaf's shape, vein pattern, or edge variation was crucial to early food gatherers. To survive, each generation relied on the experience of their elders and their own acute observation skills. Still, the eyes could be fooled, and the memory was often unreliable. A print, however, taken directly from the plant could be trusted.

Perhaps nature herself taught the first person to make leaf prints. Robert Little in his book *Nature Printing*[1] quotes Henry Bradbury, "Nature, in her mysterious operations, seems to have given the first hint upon the subject: witness the beautiful and accurate impressions of Plants to be seen in the coal-formations." Although we may not know its exact origin, we do know that even great artists like Leonardo da Vinci were intrigued by nature printing, as a description of the process appears in his fifteenth-century notes.

In America in the 1700's, early prints were probably made by holding a leaf over a candle flame or a lamp until it was coated with a thick layer of black soot. Then when it was placed between two sheets of paper and rubbed, the plant's blackened image would transfer to the paper. It was Benjamin Franklin, however, that Robert Little credits with an ingenious use of the process in 1739. Noting that the individual characteristics of a leaf impression were difficult to copy precisely, he used nature prints to foil counterfeiters. Franklin printed "three blackberry leaves on a sprig and a willow leaf with stipules" on colonial currency and then kept the method a secret. It wasn't until 1963 when an anonymous article was attributed to him that he received credit for his cleverness.

5-6 Betty Auchard painted dyes onto this assortment of plant materials and overlapped the individual images to create a bouquet composition. The first leaf was left in place on the fabric to act as a mask as the second leaf was printed over it, and so on.

Today leaf or nature printing is done mainly for artistic reasons. After your first print, you'll find it easy to understand why so many generations have found the process fascinating. You never know what is hidden on the leaf's surface until you paint and press it to the cloth.

I know that printing has changed the way I view leaves. Up until the first print, my interest had been focused on their color tones, especially fall ones. But now, I notice everything about a leaf—its outline, vein structure, even insect holes. As much as I enjoy this increased awareness, it has made walking around the block a very slow process. I have to stop and start many times as I examine each leaf for good printing qualities. I suppose my neighbors would find it amusing if I told them that I covet their leaves more than their beautiful homes. But perhaps

they know already, as I have made a lot of new friends as I trespass.

Procedure: Leaf Printing with Fabric Paints

Whether walking through a park, the woods, or your own backyard, nature's options are endless. Start by selecting leaves that have a strong vein pattern and are likely to be tough enough to withstand the printing process (oak, maple, fig). For the plant's sake, collect only as many fresh leaves as you can print in a day, as they tend to go limp or curl unless kept in the refrigerator in a plastic bag or in water. Although summer will yield the largest selection, even winter leaves found under the snow can be washed and used to produce reasonably good prints.

When traveling, many leaves will keep if you sandwich them between the pages of a

5-7 Inkodyes (see Heliotropic Printing on page 59) were painted and sprayed onto the leaves to make a rich combination of colors and textures. Later the shapes' edges and the background areas were enhanced with textile markers and brush painting to create a beautiful watercolor-like print. By Betty Auchard.

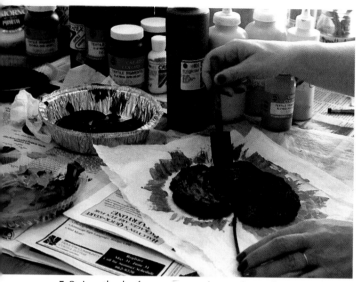

5-8 Lay the leaf on paper and coat the surface with fabric paint. One color or many may be used on the same leaf.

5-9 Hold the paper-covered leaf with one hand and gently rub the leaf's surface with the other to transfer the image to the fabric. A printer's barren may also be used to apply pressure if the leaf is large.

5-10 Lift the paper and leaf off the fabric carefully to reveal the finished nature print. If you leave the first leaf in place, it will act as a mask as you print other leaves around it to create an overlapping effect.

5-11 Detail of finished transfer

I was surprised that it was still usable. As my interest was not in the vein pattern but the leaf's bumpy surface, which had retained its moisture, I was happy with the resulting prints and the memories they evoked. (See 5-12.)

book or magazine. This will keep them flat and protected until you arrive home. Don't wait too long to print, however, as the leaf will become less flexible as it dries out.

A very fleshy leaf, however, will keep longer. When I visited Hawaii, I picked a large, thick, fuzzy leaf from a friend's garden. Wrapped in plastic wrap and placed between cardboard, it stayed in my suitcase for two weeks. When I finally unwrapped it at home,

1. Arrange all the leaves on your work table and play with different design combinations. When you've decided on a composition, read through the instructions and assemble all needed items before beginning.

2. Protect your work surface with newspapers or old sheets. Avoid plastic as it increases

50

5-12 I picked this large, fleshy heart-shaped leaf in a Hawaiian friend's garden. When I arrived home weeks later, the leaf was still good enough to print fabric. Looking at the cloth floods me with memories of the day and all the exotic plants I saw in Hawaii. Deka fabric paint on cotton/polyester fabric.

the chance of the fabric shifting. It also delays the paints' drying time. Be sure newspapers or sheets are wrinkle free or the creases will show in the leaf print.

3. Spread your washed and well-ironed fabric over the prepared surface. Smooth out the wrinkles and tape the corners down to prevent slippage. A smooth, finely woven fabric (natural or synthetic fibers) whose texture will not interfere with the delicate leaf lines works best.

4. Use fabric paints (any brand) and mix all the color combinations you plan to use. If you want light pastel colors, dilute the paint with extender, or water, or white paint. Don't use too much water, or the paint will not adhere to the leaf's

surface. If the leaf will not accept the paint at all, clean it with glass cleaner and try again.

5. Lay the leaf on clean newspaper (or other scrap paper) with the side you want to print facing you. Hold onto the stem and brush paint gently onto its surface with a bristle or foam brush. Coat it well, but not so heavily that paint pools around the veins. (See 5–8.)

6. Lift the coated leaf off the newspaper by the stem or with tweezers, if the complete stem has been painted. Tweezers for plucking eyebrows will work, but the scientific, fine-pointed types are better. Position the top end of the painted leaf face down on the fabric, holding it in place with your

fingertip while you lower the rest of the leaf to the fabric.

7. Lay a slightly larger piece of scrap paper over the leaf. The scrap paper will hold the leaf in place, absorb escaping paint, and protect your fabric from paint-stained hands. Any type of paper will work, but tissue paper allows you to see and feel the leaf as the image transfer is occurring.

8. Hold the paper-covered leaf down with one hand. With the other hand, gently rub the leaf's surface, from the center outward, to transfer the paint. A printing barren may also be used if the leaf is large. Don't rub too hard or you'll lose the fine details and cause the paint to spread beyond the leaf's edge. (See 5–9, page 50.)

Feel the contours of the leaf through the paper. Take time to enjoy each vein as it passes under your fingers—a tiny network that sustains life. Although you won't be able to see the print developing under the leaf, with practice you should be able to sense the amount of hand pressure needed. Finish the transfer by rubbing the stem. Avoid returning to a section you have already rubbed, as the leaf's placement will have shifted.

9. Lift the scrap paper's edge enough to grab the stem. Remove the leaf and the paper from the fabric at the same time. Usually, the two stick together after printing anyhow, but be sure one doesn't fall onto the newly printed fabric. The stained scrap paper should be discarded after each print. (See 5–10, page 50.)

10. Continue to repeat this process until your leaf starts to show signs of wear or flattening (anywhere from 5 to 10 prints) and then change to a new leaf. If you are printing yardage, plan your design to incorporate leaf changes, as each will vary slightly. Heat set fabric according to the manufacturer's instructions.

5-13 The leaf was printed using Jaquard fabric paint and then enhanced with Zig® textile markers. By Carolyn Dahl.

5-14 Combining leaf prints makes an interesting quilt block. Prints by Betty Auchard.

5-15 Thickened fiber reactive dyes were used by Renata Sawyer in this leaf print on silk. Photograph by Vern Sawyer.

FISH PRINTING AND GYOTAKU

At one time or another, fish have entered our lives as food, symbols, or a source of artistic inspiration. What better way to honor and remember their bounty and beauty than through a fish print.

Even though I had files bulging with fish photos, I never thought about printing directly from fish until I met Winnie Lindveit. I was teaching a silk painting workshop, and Winnie invited me to dinner and to see her art work.

I have always loved the moment just before I enter the home of someone I don't know well. Sometimes the door opens to a house that could be anyone's, but at Winnie's, it opened to her passion—the sea. Everywhere I looked, the sea seemed close by. Shells, coral chunks, crab claws filled shoe boxes stacked three high on her studio shelves. Watercolor seascapes decorated the living room and fish identification charts hung on doors. In the dining room I was treated to a full gallery of fish prints, some framed and others lying in stacks on the table like an art fish market.

That evening I learned about fish printing and the differences in techniques. Winnie, like most fish printers in the West, prefers the direct printing method. The paint is applied to the fish, the fabric (or paper) laid over it, and then the shape is transferred to the

5-16 Ann Bae Machado lives in Hawaii. When she goes for her daily swim, she often sees these beautiful flying gurnard fish leap out of the ocean and glide. Japanese oil paints on Oriental paper, indirect method. Print by Ann Bae Machado.

5-17 Fish have individual "portraits" that can be quite varied and expressive depending on their tail position, fin structure, and scale pattern. Acrylic paint on fabric, direct method. Print by Winnie Lindveit.

underside of the fabric by rubbing. Those who follow the Oriental, or indirect method, lay the fabric over a clean fish, and then dab the color onto the fabric to reveal the textured fish image; this is much like a stone rubbing. Not only can fish be printed with these two methods, but also seashells, seaweed, and other objects from the sea.

I returned to the hotel that night with more than memories of a delicious meal. I had a new process swimming in my head, two fish prints I had traded for silk, a handful of perfect sand dollars, and more than a touch of Winnie's passion. Hoping she will inspire you, here is her process for direct fish printing on fabric.

Direct Fish Printing Method

1. Go fishing. Select a beautiful spot and contemplate nature until the fish that wants to be printed arrives. Or purchase a fresh fish with scales intact at the market. Bass, flounder, and perch are good beginners' fish.

2. Remove the insides, including the gills, to prevent moisture leakage during printing. Stuff the cavity with paper towels to create volume. Sew the opening closed with a curved needle threaded with cotton thread that is doubled. Make the stitches unobtru-

sive and maintain a smooth belly line. Blot the outside of the fish with paper towels to clean and dry the surface. Apply a gentle pressure so any remaining moisture inside the fish will be released. Lay the fish on a large piece of clean wax paper placed on a hard surface such as a table or counter.

3. Level and steady the fish by placing supports made from modeling clay (or Styrofoam blocks) under the tail, fins, and mouth (Fig. 5-1). Once enough clay has been added so all parts of the fish are level, lift the tail, fins, and head just enough to slip in a piece of scrap paper on top of the clay supports to protect the clay from paint. This scrap paper will need to be changed for every print you make.

4. If a centered image is desired, determine the center of the fish with a measuring tape. Draw vertical and horizontal center lines (on the wax paper) extending out from the fish (Fig. 5-2).

5. Select a finely woven, light colored, washed and ironed fabric (a poly/cotton blend works well). Cut a square or rectangle slightly larger than the fish. Now find the fabric's center by folding the fabric in half and then in half again. The corner point created by the two folds is the center.

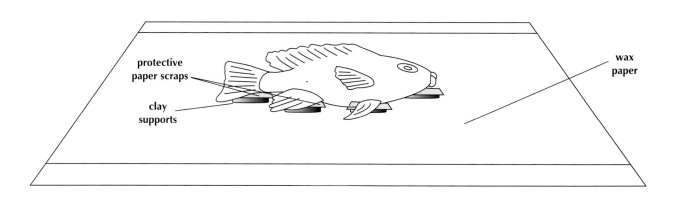

Fig. 5-1 Clay supports are placed under the tail, fins, and mouth to level and secure the fish for printing.

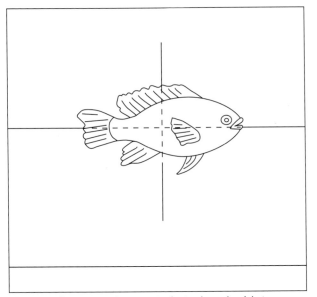

Fig. 5-2 If a centered image is desired on the fabric, determine the center of the fish with a measuring tape and draw the lines on the wax paper.

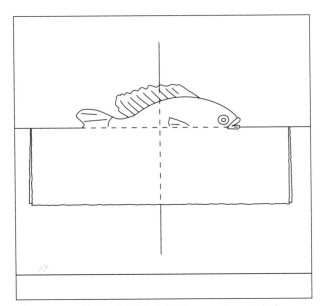

Fig. 5-3 Match the fabric's folded center line with the center lines drawn on the wax paper, unfold the fabric, and cover the fish.

Press the fold lines with your hands to make the creases easier to see. Unfold the fabric once, but leave it folded in half. Lay the fabric aside.

6. Prepare the printing colors. Winnie uses 1 part artist's acrylic paint to 1 part acrylic gel medium, diluted slightly with water until a thick painting consistency is reached. Dab the paint on the body of the fish using a foam brush. Work quickly, first brushing in the direction of the scales, and then in the reverse direction. Do not paint over the eye, which will be painted in after the print is dry. Switch to a blender brush (fan shaped) and paint the fins and tail. More than one color can be used, and glitter can be added to give a wet, irides-cent effect. After the fish has been painted, lift the parts resting on the clay supports, and carefully remove the paint-soiled scrap paper before printing.

7. Place the still folded fabric on the fish, matching the fabric's center lines with those drawn on the wax paper (Fig. 5-3). Carefully open out the last fold and cover the fish with the fabric, avoiding wrinkles or air bubbles. Gently press the fabric onto the fins, tail, belly, and head to anchor it. Begin in the center of the body and slowly rub with your hand toward the edges to transfer the paint to the fabric. Then proceed to the fins, tail, and lastly the head. If necessary repeat the process, but be sure the fabric doesn't shift or the image will be blurred. When finished, slowly lift off the fabric beginning with the head. Lay the print aside to dry. To make more prints, repeat the procedure. Experiment with varying the placement and colors, or adding elements to the background. The fish may need to be cleaned about every third print to prevent paint buildup.

8. Allow all the prints to dry completely. Now "life" must be returned to the fish by paint-ing in the eye. Because the eye was not covered with paint, it will appear as a blank circle. Once you paint the eye, the fish regains its spirit. As Winnie says "a good eye equals a good print."

9. Wait 4 to 7 days for the binder in the paint to dry completely, then iron the print on the wrong side to make the paint more permanent.

5-18 If you've already eaten your fish, you can still make a "bone print." Acrylic paint on cotton, direct method. Print by Winnie Lindveit.

5-19 The flat flounder with its two eyes on one side makes a bold print. Acrylic paint on cotton. By Winnie Lindveit.

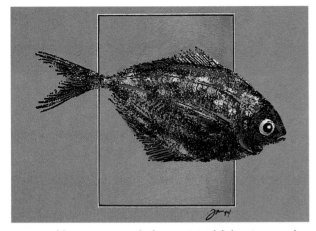

5-20 Rubber stamps made from original fish prints can be substituted if you prefer not to print from the fish directly. Print by Fred Mullett.

5-21 The inherent luster of silk makes the colors appear more luminous on this rainbow runner fish. Notice the large pupil banded by a ring of color, with a white highlight. Japanese oil paint on China silk, indirect method. Print by Ann Bae Machado.

Indirect Fish Printing Method

In Japan, the direct method of fish printing is also used, but mainly for advertising purposes. A fishing tackle store owner might decorate banners with prints done in the direct method, or sell a kit containing rub-on carbon paper for the do-it-yourself fisherman.[2] But to be a true art form, worthy of the name gyotaku (fish rubbing), a print would need to be made by the indirect method.

Supposedly invented by samurai warriors sometime in the Tokugawa Era (1600–1868), gyotaku proved not only their fishing abilities, but also their artistic capabilities. Both were required of a true samurai warrior. Few Japanese practice gyotaku today, but the numbers are growing internationally as skilled teachers revive the art form both in the East and West.[3]

Although thin Oriental paper is traditionally used, the indirect method also works on smooth silk such as habutai, or China silk. Water-based fabric paint may be used, but many artists prefer paints with an oil base. The fish is cleaned and prepared but is not painted as in the direct method, which is why some people claim that the fish can be eaten after a quick printing session. Instead, fabric (or paper) is laid over the fish and color tapped onto the fabric with a dauber (also called a tampo) in a delicate up-and-down motion. A dauber is made from a square piece of silk, filled with cotton, gathered, and closed with

rubber bands. It should feel as soft as an earlobe. It takes some practice to achieve the right pressure, but because the image appears on top of the fabric like a rubbing, you can see the results immediately. Overlapping fish images are easier to achieve with the indirect method also as you can visually gauge their placement.

A print of a fish honors not only its life but all life. Fish printers know that the availability of beautiful fish forms requires a healthy environment and a respect for species survival. Many printers are reluctant to kill

5-22 Multiple colors have been applied in a pattern to duplicate the markings of this exotic quill back fish. Japanese oil paint on China silk, indirect method. Print by Ann Bae Machado.

57

fish, especially female ones. Some printers, I've heard, even try to print from live fish. Supposedly, fish can live out of water for a short time period. If one is quick and tenacious, a fish can be painted, printed, cleaned, and returned to the water unharmed. Although I have never seen these prints, I can't imagine a fish cooperating. However, I'm sure that the result of this struggle has an in-motion beauty all its own, and the process certainly deserves admiration.

Sometimes a good printing fish is kept for years by devoted printers who make hundreds of prints from that one specimen. If the fish is wrapped in plastic carefully, with the delicate fins and tail folded in, it can be frozen. When more prints are wanted, the fish is thawed, printed, cleaned, and returned to the freezer as quickly as possible. In fact, some printers confess shyly that the same fish has lived in their freezers for as long as 6 to 8 years. But fish lovers feel it's much better to preserve a beautiful specimen than to go through many fish trying to find the same bold scale pattern or graceful tail shape.

Another option is the one Fred Mullett uses. He makes a mold of the fish from household silicone caulking, and then a plaster cast from the mold. Not only do the casts reduce the number of fish used, but also offer other advantages. They retain the details of the original fish, are always ready to use, never acquire an odor, and can be remade if broken. From these casts, Fred makes numerous fish prints on paper using oil-based inks. Best of all, he has translated his prints into rubber stamps. So if you prefer not to work directly from a fish, you can use heat transfer inks (page 88) with his fish stamps and still have the delicate beauty of an original fish print on your fabric.

5-23 A sense of depth is created in this composition by changing the stamp size, varying the colors, and placing the fish in front of the sponged shapes. Print by Fred Mullett.

HELIOTROPIC PRINTING

Even though the July heat at noon could melt the smile off my face, I'm standing on a burning concrete driveway in full sun. At my feet, a mud-gray fabric begins its metamorphosis toward purple. As the gray edges tinge with pink, I'm fascinated again by the magic of heliotropic, or sun-reactive dyes. I'm making photograms by sensitizing fabric with special dyes and then placing assorted objects on the fabric to block the sun's rays and create a pattern. The process is a lot like getting a tan. Exposed parts of the skin (the sensitized fabric) change color; the covered parts remain white.

Of course, the sun doesn't need me hovering over the fabric to do its work. But I'm reluctant to leave and miss any of the strangely hued color changes. So I bear the hot concrete just for the privilege of watching

5-24 Any object can be used in designing a photogram as long as it is opaque enough to block the sun's rays.

the pink fabric turn to lavender. Only when it ripens in the sun to the red-purple of my backyard morning glories do I leave its side for a glass of iced tea.

5-25 Paper stencils and Inkodyes were used to create the first stage of this in-process photogram.

The Dye

The dyes used to sensitize the fabric are called Inkodyes. Also known as sun-reactive or heliotropic dyes, they do not reveal their final color until exposed to sunlight or artificial ultraviolet light such as a sun lamp. Unlike the dyes used in most of this book, which are from the fiber reactive class, Inkodyes come from a different class, called vat dyes (the early fermentation process used old wine vats). They produce brilliant colors on untreated white or light color cellulose fibers such as cotton, viscose rayon, and linen. The colors are very permanent and according to the supplier can "withstand strong soaps, boiling water, rubbing, dry cleaning, common bleaches, or strong direct sunlight for a long time."[4] Inkodyes are sold as a concentrated liquid that can be diluted with water or clear extender. In light-proof plastic bottles, they can be stored in a cool, dark place for approximately one year with little color loss.

Color Mixing

Poured straight from the bottle, Inkodye resembles a grayish-white cream. This is its "leuco" form, from the Greek "leukos" meaning white. However, as soon as the dye makes contact with the air and light, it begins to change color. You don't have time to play around with color mixtures as you do with fiber reactives, nor can you judge a color by sight. As the dyes don't show their true colors until exposed to light, fabric test strips have to be made beforehand. Then when you're ready to work, you can refer to your notes and mix the proportions quickly in a dim room.

Start by making test strips of all the stock colors. Inkodyes come in red, red orange, orange, orange yellow, yellow, yellow green, green, blue green, blue, blue violet, violet, red violet, brown, and black. The dyes are transparent so the undercolor will be affected by the applied color (blue dye over yellow fabric will produce a green color).

A mixture of 1 part dye to 2 parts water (or clear extender sold by manufacturer) will yield a medium shade. Dip or paint the dye onto a fabric strip (or make a chart on one piece of cloth) and take it outside into full sun to develop. Keep notes on the proportions used, the exposure time, and fabric type. These can also be written on the fabric with permanent marker if you prefer.

If you find some of the colors too vivid, add a small amount of brown or black. If you want lighter shades (pastels), dilute the color with clear extender or with water. Adding the extender will maintain the dye's viscosity and minimize bleeding if the dye is used for stamping, stenciling, or printing. Water will dilute the dye's consistency but is a good choice for watercolor techniques, spraying, and immersing.

5-26 Once the photogram process is complete, this design could be further developed with additional techniques, such as hand painting, textile markers, and machine stitching.

Photograms

Inkodyes can be used for many techniques: direct painting, printing, compression techniques, wax resist, and warp painting. But one of the most intriguing is making photograms in the sun. A photogram is a direct contact print made by laying opaque objects on fabric that has been sensitized by soaking in Inkodye. Where the object is placed, the sun will be blocked (resisted) from reaching the light-sensitive fabric and little or no chemical reaction, or color change, will occur. When the cloth is dry and the objects are removed, their outlines will appear in the original fabric color to form the design. Those areas of the fabric not covered by an object will be exposed to the sunlight, causing the dye to react and the color to develop.

Many objects can be used to create patterns and shapes on fabric: lace, toothpicks, leaves, rocks, gutter screens, nursery plant trays, open net rug padding, opaque stencils, toys, precut cardboard and wood shapes, drafting templates, ribbon, twigs, and handcut stencils. Enlarged camera negatives may also be used, or you can make your own by drawing on mylar or acetate with opaque inks.

Materials

A sturdy board on which to transport the fabric and objects into the sun for developing (plywood, heavy cardboard, masonite, foamboard).

An assortment of objects or stencils.

Containers with lids for soaking the fabric in the dye. The container should be of nonreactive materials, such as plastic, glass, or enamel. Do not reuse containers for food preparation. Avoid very large ones, as they require too much dye.

Plastic measuring cups, spoons, fabric test strips, and your notes.

Washed fabric (cotton, viscose rayon, linen) cut to the board size or slightly smaller. The fabric may be damp, but not so wet that it dilutes the dye. No need to iron.

Weights to keep the objects from blowing off the fabric. If your objects are large, rocks, tiles, pottery shards may be used. If the objects are small and delicate, a sheet of glass or Plexiglas (without scratches) will need to be placed over the whole composition to hold the objects firmly against the fabric.

Safety equipment to wear while saturating the fabric and arranging the objects: eye goggles, rubber gloves, respirator, and long-sleeve shirt.

Procedure: Photogram Process

1. Choose a clear sunny day without clouds. The area where you plan to expose the dyes to the sun should be free of shadows and receive at least two hours of direct overhead sun (between 10 a.m. and 2 p.m. is best). The temperature needs to be at least 65°F. for the dyes to develop properly; for many geographical areas, this process will be limited to summer. You do not need to work on hot concrete as I do, but the warmth it generates seems to shorten the developing time.

2. Assemble all your work materials in a semi-dark area away from natural light. A dark basement, bathroom, or a garage with few windows work well (be sure your board will go through the door). You need to have enough interior light to work out your composition (plan it beforehand), but not enough to start your dyes reacting if you want strong color contrasts. Protect all work surfaces (counters, floors) with newspaper as the dye stains.

3. Put on the safety equipment and pour the dye and water (1 to 2 ratio) into the container. Pour out only the amount of dye you need and cap the bottle immediately. Mix the solution well and submerge the fabric in the dye, turning and squeezing the cloth to distribute the color evenly.

   When the fabric is saturated, gently squeeze out excess dye solution (remove only enough to keep it from pooling or

5-27 An assortment of heliotropic dyed fabrics. By Carolyn Dahl.

dripping off the board). Cover the dye container with the lid, or a newspaper to block out light. The fabric is now sensitized and will react to light exposure.

4. Lay the sensitized fabric on the board and smooth out wrinkles and folds. Arrange the objects on the fabric and position the weights or sheet of glass/Plexiglas. Very slowly and carefully carry the board horizontally into the sunlight.

5. The dyes will start to react immediately. The development time will vary with the climate, but expect at least 20–30 minutes in direct overhead sun. Winter sun will take longer than summer sun. Don't worry about over exposure and don't panic if some of the transitional colors are weird (but wonderful I think). Each color has its own development sequence, and eventually the color you want will appear.

6. Allow the fabric to dry in the sun. Remember, if you remove the objects or stencils while the fabric is still wet and in the sun, the once-covered areas will begin to develop. However, you can move the board to a dim area and then remove the objects (wash fabric immediately). Although direct sunlight gives the most intense colors, Inkodyes can be developed by using artificial ultraviolet (UV) light, such as sun lamps. The exposure time will be longer, however, and influenced by the age of the bulb, the distance from the work (approximately 12" to 24" is recommended), and the dye color you are using. Wear sunglasses to protect your eyes from the strong ultraviolet light.

After exposure to the sun, the dye is permanently fixed in the fabric and no additional heat setting is necessary. To remove the unreacted dye from the areas that weren't exposed to the sun, the fabric must be washed. Fill your machine with plenty of warm, soapy water and wash on a regular cycle and machine dry. I have noticed that when I use blue in strong concentrations, it sometimes rubs off on the plastic parts of my dryer. Even though it has never transferred to subsequent loads, I prefer to line dry that color.

Whenever I finish one batch of sun fabrics, I am always planning the next. The object box swells with new additions, the weather is watched, and I await the sun. During the year I studied art in Italy, I learned a word that so aptly describes my mood—*bramasole*. It means to long for, to desire, to yearn for the sun. Now I finally understand the Italian passion behind the word.

SPONGE & HEATED-FOAM PRINTING

You draw to yourself what is most in your mind, according to folk wisdom. I guess sponges are planted in mine. Ever since I began collecting sponges for fabric patterning, they have appeared all over my life.

I used to avoid the cleaning aisle in supermarkets, but now I'm fascinated by mop heads, bottle wands, squeegees, and cleaning sponges. At cosmetic counters, I purchase the newest eye-shadow applicators and sponge wedges, promising myself I'll wear more make-up. When my local five-and-dime store owner digs into a pile of objects that hasn't been disturbed in years and pulls out a fanciful bee sponge, my day is made. The drawers fill and the cupboards bulge with my collection, but there's not a sponge in the house that anyone dares use for cleaning.

Still, as much as I enjoy adding each new sponge, its discovery always shocks me somewhat. I'm surprised at how long it took me to see all the sponge forms that I now know surround me. It's startling to think about how many other things reach out to me daily, but are never noticed because I haven't put the

6-1 Needlepoint canvas served as the ground fabric in this fold dyed and sponged collage. By Carolyn Dahl.

thought of them in my mind. So maybe the value of my collection goes beyond fabric decoration. Perhaps each sponge will remind me to look a little closer, and have a greater appreciation, for all the humble objects sharing my life.

SPONGES AND PATTERNS

Most of the sponges available for fabric patterning (or sponge printing) will be of four types: animal, cellulose, synthetic, or heat-moldable foam. Each one will yield a different pattern.

Animal/Sea Sponges

When you hold a sea sponge, it's hard to believe that it is actually the remains of a primitive, multi-cellular animal. Sponges are classified as animals because they eat their food by pumping water through their body cavities to extract nutrients; whereas, plants manufacture their own food. These cavities are what account for its phylum being called *Porifera*, from the Latin word meaning pore-

bearer. Sometimes the pores are more like channels, producing a fluid pattern reminiscent of the waves that used to wash through them. At other times, they are delicate and feathery, like coral imprints. Each sponge is different, yielding its own unique pattern, like a fingerprint. Sea sponges never let you forget the origin of their beauty, however. They always manage to drop a few grains of sea sand into your hand, and to smell faintly of the sea even after years of use.

Cellulose

Most of the cleaning sponges you will find are made from cellulose. Often called "natural

6-3 An assortment of children's tile sponges. These are hard, compressed shapes that children wet and stick on shower or bath tile. Sample fabrics were printed with thickened dye.

6-2 Some of the many sponges that make up my collection. Starting at left grouping, from top to bottom: cellulose sponges cut into shapes, comb-shaped toe separator sponge, latex cosmetic wedges, pink sheet of compressed cellulose sponge, round latex sponges, foam puzzle pieces. Center column: ridge and waffle cellulose sponges, dinosaur sponge cut apart, giraffe tile sponge, foam shoe cushion. Right column: sea sponges, loofah (a dried gourd), paint roller, hair curler, foam applicator with cut edges, sponge cloth with tire-track design.

6-4 Sometimes the lack of detail in a children's sponge makes the image ambiguous and slightly haunting. This bee shape almost looks like a dog with wings.

sponges," they are made from natural materials such as cotton or wood pulp, which manufacturers process into a fiber structure, the sponge.

Because they are manufactured sponges, the pore patterns are more predictable and regular than sea sponge patterns. Although the pore shapes may not be as spontaneous looking, cellulose sponges offer other interesting options.

1. Having a dense structure, cellulose sponges are easy to modify by cutting the edge with a pair of scissors or the interior surface with an X-ACTO knife.

2. Cellulose sponges come in tightly compressed sheets that expand on contact with water into full size sponges (Ex. Design A Sponge). Because you draw your design on the dry sheet's surface and cut it out while it is flat, more precise shapes can be created.

3. Many cellulose sponges have ridges or waffle-patterned surfaces. Sponge cloth, a thin sheet sponge made to be used like a dishcloth, can be purchased in several textures. My favorite is a tire-track pattern. Cut the 6" by 7" sheet into smaller shapes, glue them onto a backing (piece of wood, cardboard, or foam board), and you have a simple printing block for adding texture. The sheet sponge can also be gathered into a dauber for applying touches of pattern in small areas or around other shapes (Fig. 6-1).

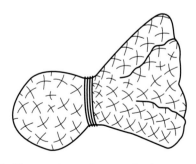

Fig. 6-1 Place a piece of sponge in the center of a square of sponge cloth. Gather the sides and secure with a rubber band to make an easy paint dauber.

Synthetic

As the name implies, these sponges are made from synthetic materials, or chemical solutions. Their printing surfaces are finely textured with few air bubbles, or none at all. Synthetic sponges are the best choice when you want your sponged shape to obscure or cover the background color or pattern, as they hold and deposit more colorant.

Most synthetic sponges are sold in cosmetic, upholstery, children's, or craft stores. Children's departments yield a lot of great animal shapes that can be used as purchased or modified. One modification method is simply to connect one section of a sponge to another section with quilter's or florist's stick pins. For example: If you pin the long tail of a dinosaur sponge to the dinosaur's back, or connect the feet, the resulting shape is unrecognizable as an animal and reads only as an abstract shape. The pin will hold fast in the rubbery texture of the sponge during printing, and when removed, the original shape is restored. You can also pin several smaller shapes together to create new designs.

Another technique is to cut the animal shape into sections. These smaller shapes can then be used individually or in combination to print designs. No one will ever suspect they started out as dinosaurs or teddy bears.

Heat-Moldable Foam Sponges

PenScore™ is a special heat-moldable foam sponge that has a closed cell structure, thus no visible pores. It is an unique material because its surface can be softened with heat and impressed with a texture. The foam block is held near a 300 to 400°F heat source (hot plate, toaster, heat gun, or iron) then pressed onto an object (pasta, button). As the hot foam cools, it becomes imprinted with the object's texture or shape. The foam block can then be used like any other sponge or stamp to print. When you've tired of that image, just heat the foam again and the pattern is erased. The foam is then ready for a new imprint. PenScore comes in three forms. The first is a PenScore™ Foam Stamp Set, composed of precut shapes such as circles, triangles, and squares that

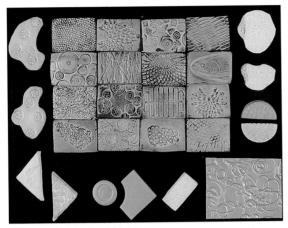

6-5 PenScore™ moldable foam sponge comes in pre-cut interlocking shapes, blue bulk blocks, and sheet stock, which can be cut into shapes.

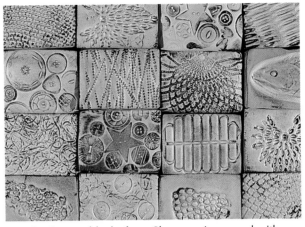

6-6 PenScore™ blocks from Clearsnap impressed with buttons, net dish cloth, potato masher, lace, coral and plastic fish.

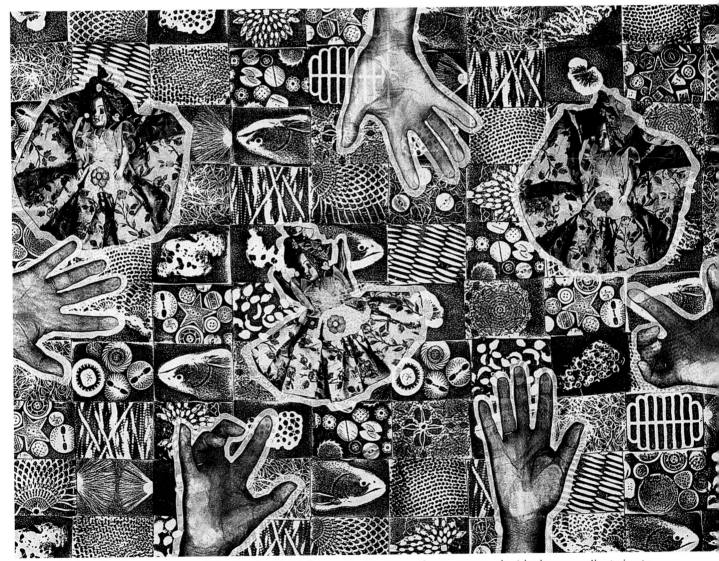

6-7 *Don't Throw Away My Dolls* by Carolyn Dahl. Every object in this quilt represents a cherished memory I'm trying to catch for safekeeping (grandmother's buttons, mother's doilies, my sister's sea coral, childhood storybook dolls).

interlock. The second is Bulk Block Stock (block foam 2³/₄" x 3³/₄" x 1¹/₄"), and the third is Sheet Stock, 8" x 10" sheets about ³/₈" thick. The sheets can be cut into shapes and mounted on wood or foam board, or left uncut for flexible printing of larger areas.

Make Samples

Whether you choose animal, cellulose, synthetic, or moldable sponges, always make a sample of each texture for design reference. Print the sponge on dry fabric and then on wet, or lightly sprayed fabric. Notice how the moisture content affects the pattern as the water disperses the color. If possible, number your sponges to match the samples. Then when it comes time to print, you don't have to wonder which sponge makes which pattern.

SPONGING PROCEDURE FOR ANIMAL, CELLULOSE, AND SYNTHETIC SPONGES

1. Wet the sponges you will be using and squeeze out excess water. Place them face down on a paper towel to drain slightly.

2. Prepare a padded surface on which to print. How thick it should be depends on your sponge. A general rule is if the sponge is hard, you need a soft surface such as a layer of felt, quilt batting, or old sheet. If the sponge is soft, the printing surface can be harder.

3. Lay your washed, ironed, and dry fabric on the printing surface. Tape the fabric to the surface at various points, to prevent shifting. If you plan to moisten the fabric by

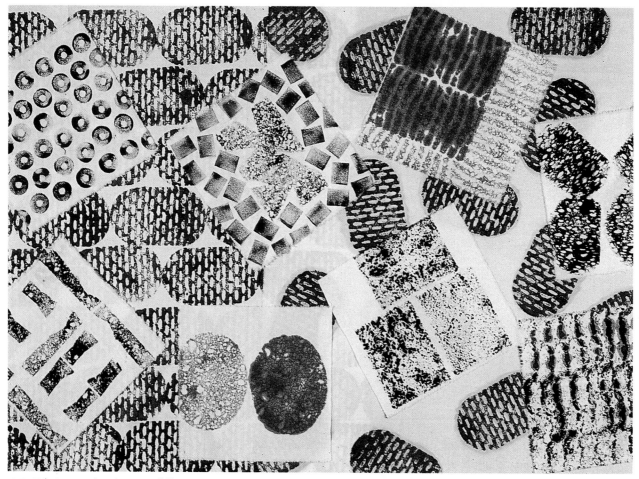

6-8 Fabric samples showing different sponge textures and the effect of moisture on some of the patterns.

spraying or brushing with water, do so now.

4. Mix the colors, using either undiluted fabric paint or thickened dyes. The colors may either be spread on a plastic tray (or piece of glass) and the sponge pressed into the color, or painted on the sponge's surface with a foam applicator or a brush.

   If the color appears too thick, spray lightly with water—a little at a time until the right consistency is reached. It will take a little practice with each sponge to get a feel for how much color needs to be applied. Always try your sponge on a scrap piece of fabric before printing onto your good fabric.

5. Place the color-loaded sponge face down on the fabric. Apply pressure evenly and lightly with the flat of your hand. If you press with your fingers, the pressure points will appear as color blobs on the fabric.

   If your sponge has a definite shape, gently press around the edges to ensure that the outline is making contact with the fabric. Don't move the sponge during this procedure or you might blur the image.

6. Lift the sponge off the fabric slowly. Use your opposite hand to hold down the fabric so it doesn't pull up with the sponge. Repeat the process as appropriate for your design.

7. If you are alternating several sponges, place the waiting ones face down on a wet paper towel to keep the color from drying in the sponge. Fabric paints will need to be lightly misted from time to time to prevent a skin from forming on the surface. When you have finished printing, wash your sponges immediately in running water to remove color. Let the sponges dry completely before storing.

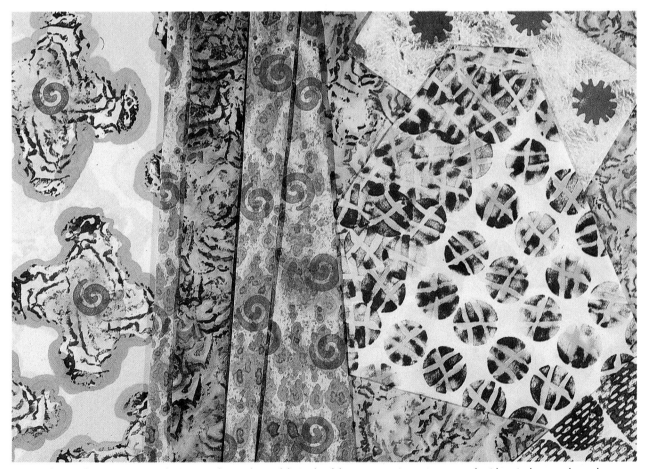

6-9 Left to right: Sea sponge design on dry and wet fabric, loofah sponge print overstamped with spirals, star-shaped sponge print on a tire-track background, latex cosmetic sponge with Oriental design, and waffle-sponged fabric.

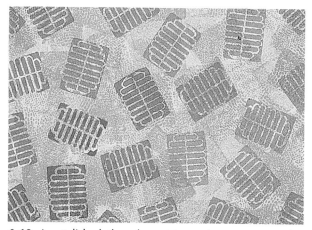

6-10 A net dish cloth and a potato masher were pressed into heat-moldable foam sponge to make these printing blocks.

6-11 The largest sponge I ever had in my collection was my "space sponge." I dyed a van load of scrap upholstery foam to create this 4' x 6' bundle, which was later sold to a museum. In contrast, the smallest sponge in my collection is only 3/8" long. It came from my eye. I was teaching "Sponging on Handwovens" at a national weavers' conference and my parting words to my students were "You never know where sponges will turn up in your life." Little did I suspect that two days later, one would be stitched to my eye during emergency surgery for retinal detachment. As it later had to be removed, it is now the most treasured part of my collection — the sponge that saved my eyesight.

6-12 Fabrics printed with cellulose sponges.

Explorations

- Overlap sponged images
- Paint multiple colors on one sponge
- Print one color on top of another
- Drag the sponge across the fabric
- Spray the print to bleed colors
- Print with a water-soluble resist instead of a colorant
- Sponge through plastic grids, open lace, stencils

Procedure for Heat-Moldable Foam Sponge

1. Hold the moldable foam (PenScore™) 4" to 6" away from a 300 to 400°F heat source (heat gun, toaster, hot plate, iron) for approximately 20 to 30 seconds. The time can vary, however. If you use the smaller blocks, less time is required to heat the surface. If you use a full sheet, more time will be needed to heat up the total surface area. Be careful not to burn yourself (gloves help) or scorch the foam.

2. Within 5 seconds, press the warm foam over a cool (room temperature) object or surface, and hold without moving for about 10 to 25 seconds. If using a piece of uncut sheet stock, place a large book over the object and foam to help distribute the pressure.

3. Lift the cooled foam off the object; its texture will be recorded in the foam. Experiment with many different objects and surfaces until you have a collection of patterns before beginning to print (pasta, rubber bands, crumpled aluminum foil, textured fabric, buttons, shells).

4. Cover work surface with a piece of craft felt or thin quilt batting to use as a printing pad. Cover pad with scrap muslin, then place washed and ironed fabric over the muslin. Smooth out wrinkles.

5. Using a small sponge, brush, or paint roller, apply fabric paint or thickened dye on the foam and print fabric.

6. Wash off foam and allow to dry. Heat the foam again for 30 to 60 seconds when you want to erase the old patterns or make additional ones. PenScore™ can also be engraved into by wetting the block or sheet slightly to prevent tearing and drawing into the surface with a ballpoint pen or pencil. These lines will not erase, however, as they are scratched into the surface instead of molded. Heat set your fabric paints according to manufacturer's instructions.

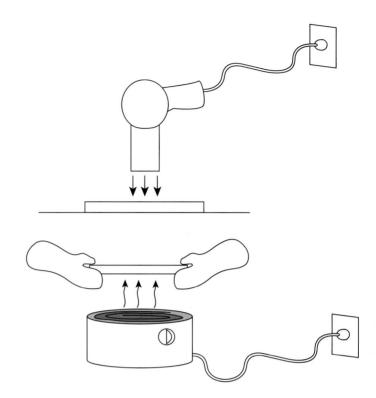

Fig. 6-2 Heat the foam for 20 to 30 seconds, using a heat gun, electric hot plate, iron, or toaster. Wear protective gloves.

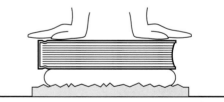

Fig. 6-3 Press the hot foam onto a textured surface. Use a large book if necessary to distribute pressure evenly.

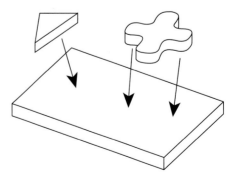

Fig. 6-4 After impressing, the sheet can be cut into smaller shapes and mounted onto a support for printing.

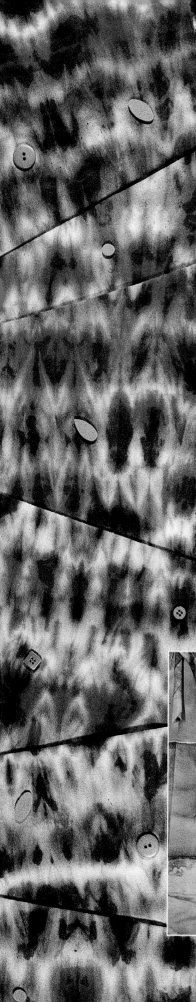

Chapter 7

COMPRESSION DYEING

*H*ave you ever tie-dyed a T-shirt, pulling up the fabric into a peak and wrapping it round and round with string? If so, you have used a compression dyeing technique. Although most people think that tie-dyeing originated in the 1960s, it is only one of the numerous compression techniques that has been used for centuries by many cultures.

In compression dyeing, the flat fabric is manipulated into a 3-D form, like the peak, which compresses the cloth into "planned wrinkles" or folds. Braiding, pleating, knotting, twisting, scrunching, folding, and stitching can all be used to squeeze the fabric together. Once in a compressed state, the fabric may need some additional bindings, such as string, rubber bands, clamps, or clothespins, to hold its dimensional form during the dyeing and drying stages.

The ready-to-dye fabric is quite beautiful, like small sculptures. It may be covered in fingerlike projections, resemble an origami folded package, look like a bumpy bundle, be stiff like a rope, or twist like a branch. But each shape has a purpose: it blocks, directs, or admits the dye into the creases. Whether the chosen pattern is quite simple, like those in this chapter, or complex enough to require a lifetime to perfect, each will have the softly defined shapes with feathered edges characteristic of all compression techniques.

Even though this method of dyeing is centuries old, few countries have given names to the patterns, except for the Japanese. The word *shibori* is perhaps a term you have already heard. It refers to the body of compression (or shape-resisted) techniques. Shibori has no

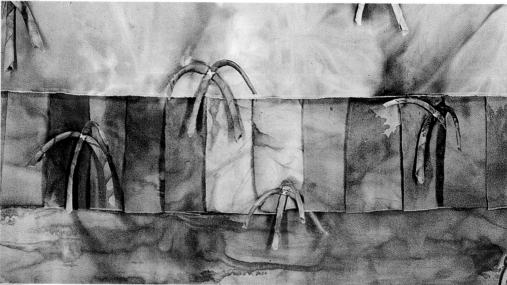

7-1 Detail of silkwork ***Shibori Storm*** by Carolyn Dahl.

English equivalent, but according to the authors of the book *Shibori*, "the word comes from the verb root *shiboru*, 'to wring, squeeze, press'...the word emphasizes the action performed on the cloth, the process of manipulating fabric."[1]

That's a definition to remember because the physical action is the key to the technique's beauty. It is also the way to read the fabric. With experience, it is possible to look at compression dyed cloth and mentally reconstruct its former dimensional shape. The cloth never forgets. Within the finished pattern, the action of the dyer's hands can always be traced.

Sometimes, however, as in very old Japanese shibori fabrics, the patterns are so complex that they cannot be understood or reproduced immediately. I'm glad they can't. For as long as dyers are interested in solving the puzzles left in these old textiles, the better the chances that the techniques will survive.

Unfortunately, as the years pass, we lose more and more master craftspeople. Many die without leaving successors, taking with them the experience of generations of dyers. The young people of most countries that produce handcrafted textiles no longer want to follow their ancestors' traditions and methods. The sad fact is that we live in a fast-paced, commercial world that seldom respects or properly rewards the dedication, hard physical labor, and creativity of cloth-making humans. Thus it's important that all of us, the fabric lovers, carry the mystery, the knowledge, and our spirit to the next set of hands.

TECHNIQUES

This chapter describes six simple methods. When you understand their use of compression, dimension, and dyeing, find a book on Japanese shibori to see what wondrous, complex design possibilities await you. See if you can read the old patterns caught in the fabric's memory.

BRAIDING

Anyone who ever wore braids as a child knows firsthand what a compression technique feels like. My scalp still tingles remembering the pulling and tugging as great handfuls of hair disappeared into skinny little whips. Now, whenever I braid fabric, I feel a special empathy for the cloth. After all, it's the only surface design technique I've ever tried on my own body.

Braiding the Fabric

1. Cut washed fabric (white or light colored cotton, silk, or rayon) into three or more equal strips approximately 6" to 8" wide. A greater width can be used, but the dye will be less likely to reach the innermost folds. The length of the strips should be approximately 1 to 1¼ yards long. If longer lengths are used, roll the ends into bobbins to prevent tangling while braiding.

2. Hold the strips together and wrap a rubber

7-2 The fabric for this silk ensemble was dyed using the compression technique of scrunching. By Carolyn Dahl.

73

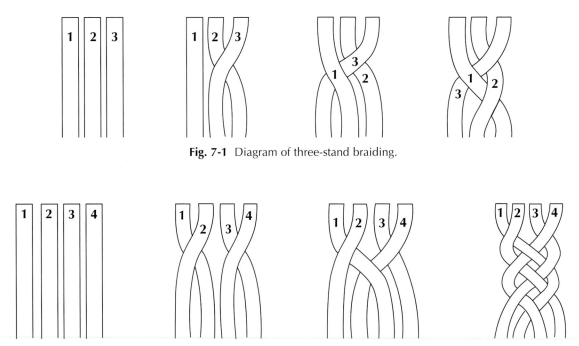

Fig. 7-1 Diagram of three-stand braiding.

Fig. 7-2 Diagram of four-strand braiding.

band several times around them, about 1 to 1½" from the end. Then slip one loop of the band over the doorknob of a closed door. The knob acts as a hook so you can pull on the fabric as you braid. An armchair leg, a bedpost, or even your foot could also be used as an anchor.

3. Begin braiding at the doorknob. Don't worry about how the material is gathering or folding, just maintain an even tension. When the braid is finished, secure the end with another rubber band (Fig. 7-1 and 7-2).

Painting the Braid

In most traditional methods, the compressed fabric is immersed in dye, usually indigo (a vat dye) which coats the fibers a deep blue. As we are using a direct application method (painting on the dye), and a different class of dyes (fiber reactive dyes), the results will vary slightly from those achieved with traditional immersion techniques. The dyes will also be thickened to slow their progress through the fabric folds and to create crisper shapes. Without some thickening, fiber reactive dyes migrate too quickly and obliterate some of the pattern.

Think of a braid as a dimensional object, composed of four painting surfaces: the top, the bottom, the right side, and the left side. Because the cloth strips have been interlaced, each strand will appear on the top surface, disappear to the bottom, come around the sides, and reappear on top again. If red dye is painted across the top of the braid, only the fabric strips that happen to be on top at that time will receive the color. Also, just as many individual hairs make up each hair braid, many fabric folds make up each strand of the cloth. Thus the red dye would also only make contact with those fabric creases facing outward on the braid.

1. Before painting, immerse the braid in water for 2 to 5 minutes (depends on the braid thickness). Squeeze out the excess water and allow to drain on a towel. Wetting the braid will drive out the air molecules filling the capillary spaces of the dry fabric and allow the liquid dye to be absorbed more readily.

2. Prepare thickened fiber reactive dyes (page 22) in the colors you will use and thin to suit your fabric. Mix your dye solutions fairly strong as the moisture in the braid

will dilute the colors somewhat. Paint some test braids first to see how quickly the dye penetrates the fabric and how thick your dye paste should be. In general, dye penetrates fabric easier (a) when the fabric is thinner and smoother rather than thicker and coarser, (b) when the braid tension is looser rather than tighter, (c) when the fabric is wetter versus drier, and (d) when the dye solution is thinner rather than thicker.

For example, if your test braid has too many white, undyed areas, you need to thin your dye or wet the braid more so the color will spread deeper into the folds. If, however, the braid pattern is weak with all the colors blurred together, you need to increase your tension while braiding and use a thicker dye solution so it won't migrate so far.

3. Activate the thickened dye, (or presoak the braids in washing soda solution, see page 18). Lay the braid on plastic. Wearing rubber gloves, paint on the dye with a brush or foam rubber applicator using some of these techniques (see 7-3).

• Paint the top of the braid one color, the bottom another, and the two sides a third color.

• Paint a light color on the top and side surfaces. Turn the braid over and paint the former bottom surface a dark color. Leave the braid in this position to dry. The dark color will migrate down into the lighter areas.

• Paint bands of one color around the circumference of a braid, spaced 1/2 to 1" apart along its length. Select a color that was mixed with several other colors. The moisture in the braid will pull the individual colors out of the painted bands and into the white areas.

• Paint bands of alternating colors several inches apart. Allow the colors to bleed a bit. Then paint the remaining light areas with another color.

• Using a fan-shaped blending brush, or

7-3 Fabric braids (three strands) painted with thickened fiber reactive dyes.

any beat-up brush that will tend to give a scratchy application, lightly drag one color of dye across the four sides of the braid. Barely touch the surface, leaving a trail of irregular lines. Repeat with a second, then a third color. As the wet braid dries, these marks will blend to create additional colors. The final effect will be a spotty pattern against a mostly white background.

• Paint the braid anyway you want. Let it dry. Open the braid and spread out the creases. Braid and paint the strips again (see 7-4 on page 76). Sometimes the braid itself is so beautiful that you may want to use it as an embellishment (see 7-5 on page 77).

TWISTING, KNOTTING, AND BINDING

These three techniques do not compress the fabric as tightly as braiding. In binding and knotting, the compression occurs only at intervals wherever the knot, rubber band, or

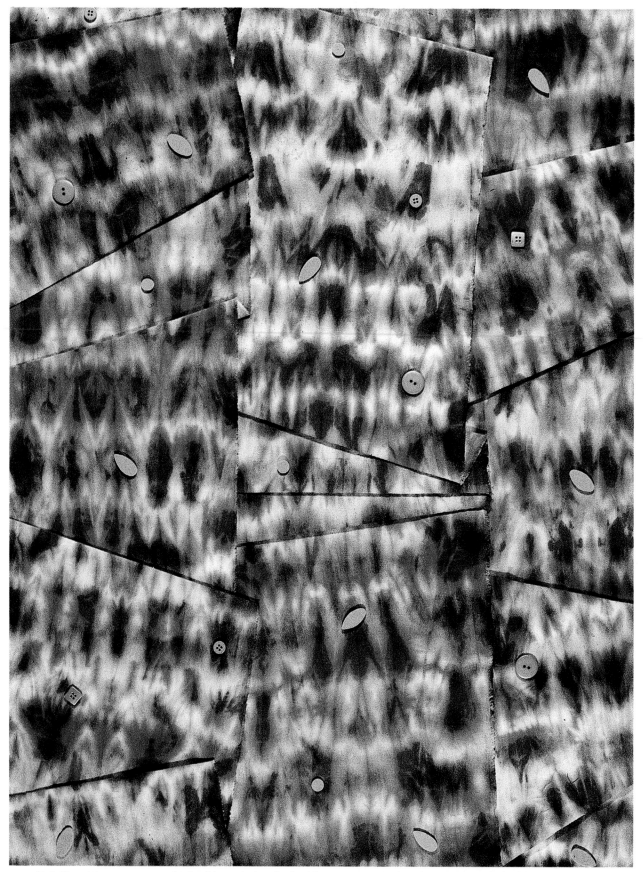

7-4 The rich pattern was obtained by painting the braid, opening it up, braiding it again, and adding new colors.

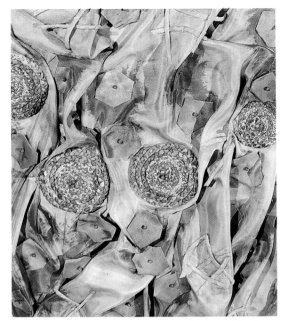

7-5 Strands of fabric previously braid dyed were combined into a new braid and used as embellishment on a discharged fabric. Detail of silkwork **Spaces Between the Flames** by Carolyn Dahl. Photograph by Michael McCormick.

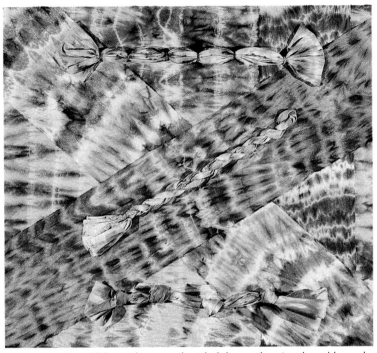

7-6 Examples of fabrics that were braided, knotted, twisted, and bound before dyeing.

other binding occurs, leaving much of the fabric loosely gathered. The action of twisting fabric forms soft folds that resist the dye only slightly. Because the dye is able to move further into the inner folds of these 3-D shapes, wider pieces of cloth may be used (see 7-6 and Fig. 7-3).

TWISTING: Hold one end of a piece of wet fabric in each hand. Begin twisting until the fabric curls back on itself (Fig. 7-4). Wrap a rubber band around the two ends to secure the twist. If the twist goes slack in the center, you may need to tie a string around that area, or wrap the twisted fabric around a cardboard tube and secure. Twisted fabric can be painted with the same methods as the braids.

KNOTTING: Make knots wherever you want on a single layer of fabric, or knot a length

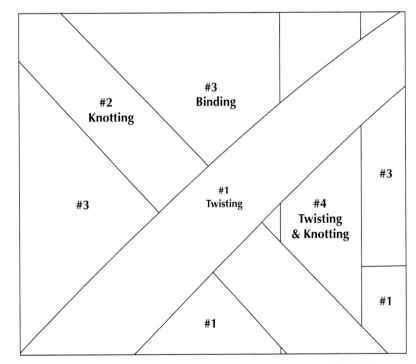

Fig. 7-3 Diagram identifies the compression techniques used in the photograph shown above.

77

Twisting

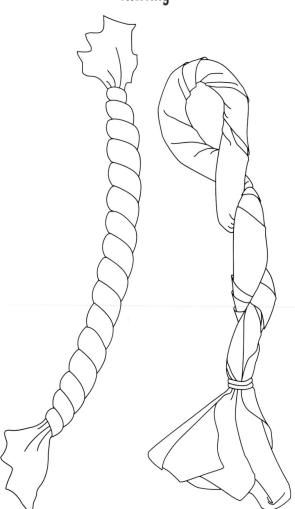

Fig. 7-4 Twist fabric until it curls back on itself. Twist will relax slightly.

Knotting

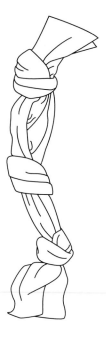

Fig. 7-5 Loosely gather fabric and make knots along length.

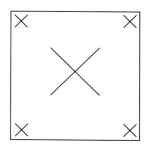

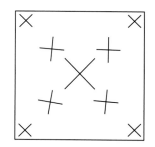

Fig. 7-6 On a single layer of fabric, pull up points and knot.

Binding

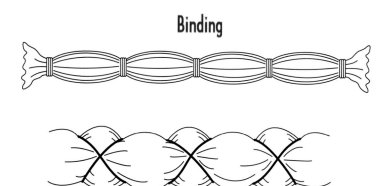

Fig. 7-7 Binding the fabric at intervals.

of slightly gathered fabric. The knots must be tight enough to block some of the dye, but loose enough to be untied later. Wet the fabric and paint one or many colors on or around the knots. Sometimes interesting effects happen if you hang or drape the fabric so the dyes will bleed in one direction (Fig. 7-5, left, and 7-6, page 77).

BINDING: A width of up to 24" can easily be dyed with the binding technique if sufficient dye is used. First pleat (or loosely gather) the wet fabric to reduce its bulk. Place rubber bands around the top and bottom ends to hold the pleats in place. Then add additional bindings (rubber bands, twist ties, dental floss, string) along the pleated fabric at intervals of approximately 2 to 3", or in spiral or crisscross patterns across the length. Paint the fabric. Not only will the pleats cause a pattern but also where the bindings cross the fabric and block the dye (Fig. 7-7, page 78).

SCRUNCHING

The random pattern produced by this method gives a mottled or marbled effect. The wet fabric is scrunched into a bundle and held tightly together with rubber bands or strings. The dye can then be painted, dripped, or poured onto the bundle. Other variations are to contain the scrunched fabric in a nylon stocking or to compress it in a small glass jar for dyeing. Once dry, the fabric can be opened up, and if desired, scrunched and dyed again (Fig. 7-8).

Drying the Fabric: Do Not Open

The fabric must be allowed to dry in its compressed dimensional shape. Resist the temptation to untie or open up the folds to sneak a peek at its progress. If the dimensional shape is undone while the fabric is still wet, the dyes will bleed into the previously unexposed areas. Your pattern will become

Fig. 7-8 Either the whole piece or a section of the fabric can be scrunched and bound before dyeing.

less defined, or perhaps lost entirely. Some very large wet braids will take 2 to 3 days to dry, although a fan can shorten the drying time. Do not undo the fabric until it is completely dry, or very nearly dry.

If the fabric is allowed to dry slowly, the MX series of dyes will have batch set. If the fabric dried quickly, or you are using the H series, you will need to set the dyes with heat.

When rinsing, do a first rinse while the fabric is still in its dimensional shape. Then open it up and wash according to the instructions for the fiber type.

Once you've mastered these basic compression shaping and dyeing techniques, you might want to invent your own variations by tying exotic Oriental knots, twisting or wrapping the fabric around various objects (tubes, ropes), binding with unusual materials, or creating braids out of four, five, or six strands.

7-7 *Shibori Storm* silkwork by Carolyn Dahl. Techniques used to pattern the fabric were pleating, binding, rolling, and scrunching. Photograph by Charlotte Cosgrove and Helen Orman.

7-8 Compressing the fabric into irregular pleats created the lines in this *Earth Strata* silkwork by Carolyn Dahl. Photograph by Michael McCormick.

STITCH AND DYE

Hotel sewing kits—I can't resist them. I leave the shower cap in its plastic wrapper, ignore the shampoo, use half of the lotion, but always take the kit with me. Why do I want it? A few bands of thread, a white button or two, a needle, a tiny pair of scissors tucked into a matchbook. These are hardly coveted materials. But—I'm a textile artist. I claim thread and collect my tools wherever I find them. No matter their actual worth. The scissors may be almost useless, the button plain, the thread boring. But they are my life's symbols, with value beyond function. I have to tuck them in my suitcase and fly them home.

What is it about stitching that so fascinates me? A needle pierces the cloth and pulls a colored thread along behind it. But something in that broken, in-and-out, dot-to-dot line appeals and satisfies. My eye can follow the thread for hours as batting gets stitched to quilts, buttons to cloth, sleeves to coats, and sequins to gowns.

Yet stitching intrigues me for another reason. So many times as I've ripped out a misplaced row of stitches, or removed an appliquéd fabric shape, I've been captivated by the beauty of the empty hole pattern. Like little bird feet walking across the cloth, the tracks of the removed thread invite my eye to follow. Perhaps these phantom stitches are why the stitch-and-dye method is one of my favorites: the pattern is caused by stitches but the design isn't revealed until the stitches are removed.

Instead of braiding or binding the fabric, stitches are pulled into tight gathers which resist the dye. In Indonesia, the method is called *tritik*, or "stitch resist." Unlike other compression techniques, which yield more textural designs, stitching can be used to achieve definite shapes, such as triangles, stars, flower shapes, etc.

This method also has another plus—it's

7-9 Different dyes and application methods will create slightly different effects even though the stitched pattern is the same. Mary Ann Willey's fabrics were immersed in indigo dye which gives a definite stitched line on a beautiful deep blue background.

portable. I have often envied stitchers working away in airports, making use of their waiting time. So many dyeing and painting techniques require the materials of a full studio. But now, I too can stitch quietly while I travel, undisturbed by anyone because they think they know what I'm doing. However, when I suddenly pull up my "quilting" into a lumpy, gathered mass, I do get puzzled and appalled looks, and sometimes seat changing.

Still the stitch-and-gather method is the perfect travel companion. Even if I've forgotten my materials at home, and the creative urge strikes in some lonely hotel room, I can always turn to the handy little sewing kit a bathroom away. It works just fine to stitch designs into any number of things in my suitcase.

Besides, it's kind of comforting. Every other item in the room feels anonymous. But a sewing kit makes you feel at home. I worry, though, that its days in the gift basket are numbered. We need to show management that its kits are still noticed by guests. So use it, or take it home. We don't want the hotel sewing kit to become another "remember when" item in our culture.

7-10 Half of a symmetrical design was stitched onto folded fabric, gathered, and painted. When the fabric was unfolded, a mirror image appeared.

Process Considerations

THE DESIGN: The design is drawn on the fabric with a soft pencil. It can be as simple as a series of straight lines or as complex as a branch of flowers. When choosing a design, remember that you must be able to pull up and gather each line or shape separately. So draw your pattern on paper first and mentally decide where each stitched line will begin and end.

NEEDLE: Select a fairly long needle, with a large eye to accommodate doubled thread, and a small sharp point to get through the layers of fabric without leaving large holes. Embroidery and crewel needles are good choices.

THE THREAD: The major consideration when choosing thread is that it be strong enough to withstand pulling without breaking. The thread should also be suitable for the weight of the fabric. Thus a lightweight silk

fabric would need a lighter weight thread such as doubled quilting thread; whereas, cotton or rayon fabric could be stitched with a thicker thread such as doubled carpet, home decorating, or upholstery thread.

THE STITCH: The most common stitch is the simple running stitch done either on the flat fabric or folded fabric. However, an overcast (over stitch) can also be used, but it is only done over the edge of a folded fabric. It's best to use a long needle for overcasting as the fabric collects on the needle as you go, and is then pushed back over the needle's eye onto the thread.

The stitch length can vary from small to medium to suit your design. A large stitch can be used for certain effects, but it will not resist the dye as well. The stitch length may be consistent or change size within the line. Usually the stitching is done parallel to the weft so you don't have to work with long lengths of thread that may tangle. However, you can stitch in any direction you want for the process to work.

THE FABRIC: Closely-woven fabric is more suitable for stitch-and-dye patterns, but open weaves will also create interesting, although less precise designs. If the design is stitched on a single layer of cloth, you will, of course, get one image. If done on folded cloth, several images or a mirror image will result depending on how the design was traced on the fabric. With some very fine fabrics, such as a delicate silk, multiple layers can be stitched at one time.

THE GATHERS: When the stitched line is pulled up, the gathers must be very tight and secured with a firm knot. You should not be able to see the thread between the folds. As this process can be very hard on the hands, well-placed bandages can keep the thread from cutting into your fingers.

THE DYE: Different classes of dyes and application methods will give slightly different results even though the same stitching procedure is used. As with the other compression techniques, we will be painting on fiber reactive dyes that have been thickened to slow and control their movement through the folds.

Stitch-and-Dye Procedure

1. Trace the design on the fabric with a soft leaded pencil, such as #2, or an Ebony pencil.

2. Thread the needle with a strong thread, doubled and knotted at the end so it won't pull through the hole left by the needle.

3. Sew along your design lines using a running stitch or an overcasting stitch on a folded edge. At the end of the row or shape, cut the thread leaving a 2" to 3" tail. Knot this end immediately so the thread doesn't slip out as you continue to work the remaining fabric.

4. When you have completed the stitching, pull on the threads to gather the fabric into tight folds. The amount of compression

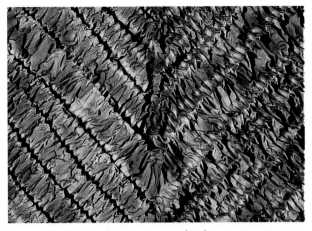

7-11 After the stitches are removed, take a moment to enjoy the beautiful topography of the fabric.

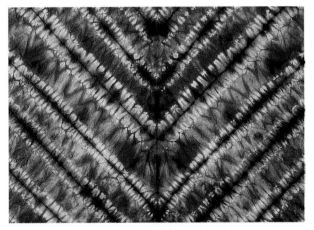

7-12 The finished stitch-dyed fabric after heat setting, washing, and ironing.

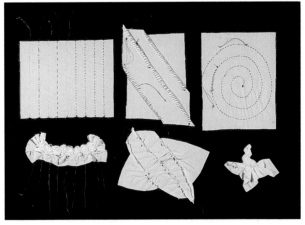

7-13 White fabric has been stitched and gathered before coloring. In the sample on the left, the different colored threads indicate that some lines will be gathered for the first coloring and others for the second coloring. In the center sample, diagonal folds have been over stitched. Running stitches can move in any direction, as in the spiral shape found in the fabric sample on the right.

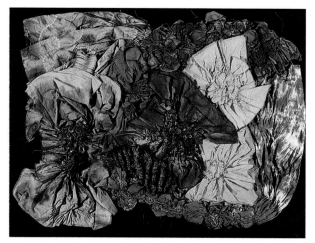

7-14 An assortment of stitched and gathered fabrics after painting with dyes.

7-15 The fabric was first hand painted in pinks and purples and then stitched and gathered. The stitching will protect some of the hand-painted colors, when a second dye is added.

determines how much dye will penetrate the fabric. With some stencil designs that have many curves, and with long overcast lines, you may need to pull up sections slightly as you go along to make it easier to gather later.

5. When all the stitched lines have been gathered, cut the thread off the needle. Separate the doubled thread into two strands and tie the ends into a tight knot to secure the gathers.

6. Wet the stitched and gathered fabric. Paint on one or many colors of the thickened fiber reactive dyes. Try not to force the dye under the stitches by dabbing with the brush too hard, or over saturating the fabric around the stitches.

7. Allow the fabric to dry completely in its dimensional form. Batch or heat set depending on the dye series used. After setting, rinse the still gathered fabric thoroughly to remove excess dye so it doesn't come off on your hands as you remove the thread.

8. Remove the stitches when the fabric is wet or dry. Use small scissors with thin blades. A seam ripper will work, but be careful not to stab a hole in the fabric. Proceed slowly and use a good light to help locate the threads and avoid cutting the fabric. I find it

easiest to clip off the knots first. This releases the gathers somewhat so I can cut or pull out the loose threads with less effort.

9. When all the stitches have been removed, you'll be treated not only to the wonderful patterns that developed within the folds, but also the "stitch tracks." The topography of the fabric is so interesting and beautiful at this point that I often wait weeks before I proceed to the next step. Finally, however, I reluctantly plunge the bumpy fabric into soapy water for its final wash and rinse. As I iron it flat, however, I can still see traces of its former dimensional self in the pattern and tiny wrinkles.

Stitch-and-Stencil Process

Quilting stencils make excellent templates for stitch-dyed designs. Most stencil designs can be traced onto the fabric and stitched as is. Some, however, will need to be modified slightly. Trace the stencil first on paper and analyze the shape. If lines overlap or are too close, if shapes run together and do not form individual units, or if the line is too long to gather, you will need to adjust the design. Taking a little time to think through the process, and marking the changes on paper first, will ensure that the stencil you've selected will work well with the stitch-and-dye method (Fig. 7-9, right).

The stencil design can either be stitched

on a single layer of fabric or a folded fabric. Stitching on one layer will result in a less defined stitched design, but many wonderful fold patterns. However, if one stitches again over the lines during quilting, the stitched pattern once again dominates the fold pattern.

If the stencil design is used on folded fabric, only half of the design needs to be traced onto the fabric. The stencil used must be symmetrical, as the final result is a mirror image of the design. Begin by folding the

fabric in half. Lay the stencil on the fabric with the fold line running down the center of the stencil. Trace only half of the stencil design onto the fabric (Fig. 7-10). Remove the stencil, connect any gaps in the lines, and pin the fabric together so it will stay folded while stitching. Starting and ending at the fabric fold, stitch over the half-design going through both layers (Fig. 7-11). Gather up the threads, and paint the bundle. When opened and unfolded, the two sides of the stencil design will join to form one shape.

Fig. 7-10 The center line of the stencil is matched to the fold line of the fabric. Only half of the stencil design is traced onto the folded fabric (stencil from The Stencil Company).

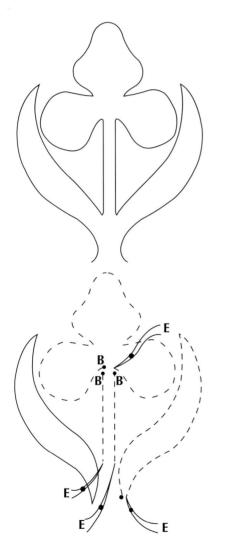

Fig. 7-9 The original quilt stencil design needed a few modifications to be used as a stitched design. The flower shape was divided into individual sections (flower head, stem, leaves) that could be gathered as units. Also, the leaf shapes were moved slightly away from the flower head for greater design clarity (stencil from The Stencil Company).

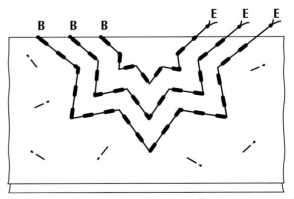

Fig. 7-11 Beginning and ending at the fold line, the traced lines are stitched through both layers of fabric. The fabric is now ready to be gathered, secured, and painted.

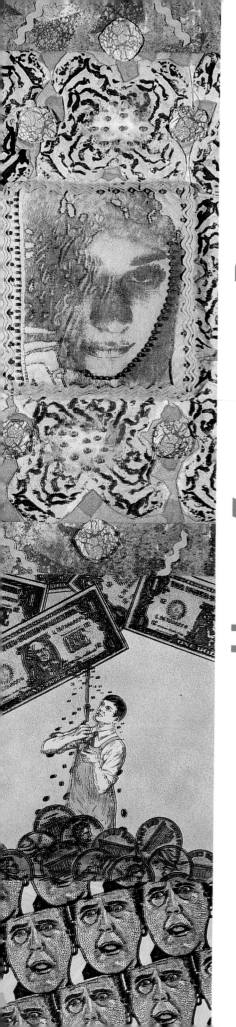

Chapter 8

HEAT TRANSFER DYES

*E*very so often, I find an old embroidery project tucked away in some long forgotten box. The metal hoop has rusted around the dusty fabric making me wonder how old I was when these half-finished flowers were started—eight, nine? What called me away so quickly that I left the still-threaded needle dangling?

I remember spending hours in Woolworth's in front of the colorful cubicles of DMC thread trying to decide which iron-on embroidery pattern I should purchase. I never could decide if my pillowcase needed birds, pansies, a cat, or a puppy with a raised paw. Usually I bought a few of each, as I still do. I guess in the end, it really didn't matter. I seldom finished any of these projects, but I still have stacks of fabric bearing the blue lines of my good intentions.

I didn't know at the time that these iron-on designs awaiting threads were a form of heat transfer printing. All I knew back then was the magic I still feel—ironing over a piece of paper and finding flowers on my fabric.

HISTORY

The earliest embroidery transfers were composed of printing inks that contained shellac and a colored pigment, usually ultramarine, which gave the characteristic blue-colored lines. More modern forms of

8-1 *The Eye in I* detail, by Carolyn Dahl.

heat transfers evolved when dyers tried to solve the problem of how to color the new man-made fabrics. Up until then, most dyeing processes were for natural fibers, which absorbed dye from a water medium. Man-made fabrics, however, were not absorbent, and new dye classes and methods had to be found. One of the results of this search was the dispersed (or disperse) dyes developed in 1923, which are used today for most design transfer methods using heat.

Although dispersed dyes solved the problem of how to color man-made fibers, some types of this dye had an annoying characteristic. When the newly dyed fabric was dried with high heat, the dye would vaporize into a gas, float around in the drying chamber, and redeposit on the finished yardage as unwanted specks of color. But as often happens when creative individuals work to correct a problem, the annoyance becomes a new technique.

In 1958, Noel De Plasse discovered that he could make use of this defect by printing patterns with the dye onto paper, laying the paper face down on the fabric, and applying heat to the backside of the paper to vaporize the dye into a gaseous state. Because the vaporized dye was sandwiched between the paper and fabric, it couldn't escape, but would cool and condense onto the fabric according to the design printed on the paper. This new method became known as heat transfer printing.[1]

It wasn't until about 1968, however, when the first industrial transfer paper was manufactured under the tradename of Sublistatic, that this new process was used to its full commercial capacity. Although most dyers refer to the method as heat transfer printing, you may find references to it as "sublistatic printing" after the paper's tradename, or "sublimation printing" after its chemical action (turning from a solid to a gaseous state to a solid without liquefying). Whatever it is called, the new technique made it possible to print intricate patterns in rich colors on man-made fabrics. Perhaps some of the best examples of the lavish surfaces this method could produce are the heavily patterned polyester shirts of the 1970s.

IMPORTANT FACTORS

I've included this chapter on the dispersed class of dyes (heat transfer dyes), as they offer the ability to produce on fabric many design possibilities that would be difficult to execute with other techniques on the soft, textural surface of cloth (precise lines, detailed stamps, rubbings, realistic drawings, paintings, photographs).

As the most crucial point in using these dyes is the moment of transfer, four materials must interact correctly for your dye to "sublime" and for a successful heat transfer to occur: the paper, the fabric, the heat source, and the dye.

8-2 Mini yardage patterned with rubber stamps and dye transfer inks. *All stamp images are copyrighted: strawberry, rose with face, the X, heart-shaped earth by Inkadinkado; armadillo, accordion, Siamese cat, and leopard by The Stamp Pad Co.; frog by Pelle's; candle by Stampendous Inc.; snakeskin and gravel rollagraphs by Clearsnap, Inc.; icicles, textured geometric shapes, morning glory by Hampton Art Stamps.*

1. **THE PAPER:** In choosing paper to use as the transfer paper, look for one that isn't very absorbent. You want the fine dye particles to adhere to the paper's surface, but not disappear into its fibers. The paper must be able to release the dye when heated. Many types of smooth, nontextured drawing papers work, as does typing paper for small projects. The paper should not be too thick or the iron's heat will not be able to penetrate, or too thin or it will wrinkle from the paint's moisture.

2. **THE FABRIC:** Dispersed dyes were developed for use on man-made fabrics (polyester, acrylic, nylon, or acetate). The greatest permanence and brightest colors are obtained on white, finely woven, 100 percent polyester fabric. Blends will also give fairly good results, as long as you select one with a high percentage of polyester. One of my favorites is a broadcloth of 65 percent polyester and 35 percent cotton. With this fiber blend, I get good transfer quality because of the high polyester content, but the fabric still has a cotton-like feel.

3. **THE HEAT SOURCE:** Whatever man-made fabric you use, it must be able to withstand the prolonged heat of a hot iron or commercial heat press. The fabric must not scorch or damage when subjected to the 350° to 400°F heat of a "cotton" or hot iron setting. Irons do vary in temperature, however. Test a swatch of your fabric by placing a piece of tissue paper over the surface and iron slowly for approximately 25 to 30 seconds. If the fabric scorches or turns brittle, adjust the iron temperature or select another fabric.

4. **THE DYE:** The heat transfer dye is found in many different forms: as a stamping ink, wax crayons, marker pens, dye sheets, ready-to-use paint, and as a powder to mix yourself. The color you see when you apply it to the paper will be different from the color on the finished fabric. In whatever form you choose to use the dye, it's best to make a timed test strip of each color to see the change after the iron's heat. When the transfer process is completed, the colors are permanent and no further heat setting is necessary. The finished fabric remains soft to the touch and can be dry cleaned or gently washed (allow at least 24 hours) and line dried.

DYE TRANSFER INK STAMP PADS

A rubber stamp supplier's catalog seems like a scrapbook to me. Images pop off every page and trigger so many personal memories. Looking at a Siamese cat stamp, I remember my "Tajma" whose gentle love accompanied me through so many tedious studio days. Occasionally, I think I still glimpse her turquoise eyes slipping around a corner.

On another page, the sight of an accordion stamp returns me to being eight years old, holding my little red accordion as my teacher called out in his Swedish accent, *Dragspel Valsen* (the *Accordion Waltz*) or *Varen Polka* (the *Springtime Polka*).

Further on, I admire a complex rendering of an armadillo stamp. The first armadillo I saw was through the glass of my grandmother's china cabinet. Curled up, with its tail in its mouth, the armadillo basket had arrived in Minnesota from my uncle who was in the Army in Texas.

When a stamp draws strong memories out of me, I have to own it and try it on fabric. But memories can be expensive once you are inside a well-stocked stamp store or browsing through a tantalizing catalog. In the beginning, I purchased many stamps that simply would not work on fabric using the traditional fabric colorants. But when I discovered dye transfer inks, I could once again purchase freely. Almost every image, even the most detailed stamp, can be transferred to a smooth fabric with these inks.

Dye transfer inks come in pre-inked stamp pads, in 12 ready-to-use colors. They can also be purchased in bottles to refill the pads or to mix custom colors to pour onto a pad without ink. The stamp is tapped on the pad and then pressed onto a piece of paper,

8-3 Stamped collages can create incongruous, unusual image combinations. Use them to express your humor as Mark Jetton did in this stamped composition. *Copyrighted images: man with drill by Fruit Basket Upset, dollars and pennies by Good Stamps.*

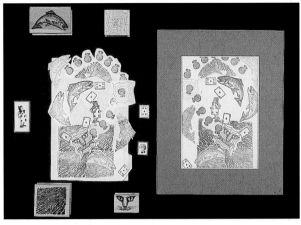

8-4 The collage consists of images that were stamped on typing paper and cut out, arranged into a composition, lightly glued to a base paper with glue stick, and then ironed to the fabric as one sheet. *All stamp images are copyrighted: rainbow trout, catface by All Night Media; spider web, oyster, playing card, and card man by Inkadinkado; sand drifts by The Stamp Pad Co.*

which becomes the "transfer paper." Any images that come out poorly, can be discarded and stamped again. Your mistakes are made on the paper, not the fabric. The transfer paper is placed stamped side down on the fabric, and ironed to transfer the images to the cloth.

You can repeat the same stamped image across the paper and iron the whole sheet for mini yardage (see 8-2). Or stamp different images on paper, cut them out, and arrange them on the fabric composing the design as you iron. Even complex collages can be created as the paper allows you to add elements, texture backgrounds, and experiment with unusual or humorous arrangements before ironing the design to the fabric (see 8-3, 8-4, 8-5).

8-5 When stamped images are combined with other techniques such as sponging and marbling, a lot of textural variety can be achieved with only a few images. Composition by Mark Jetton. *Copyrighted images: surprised man by Ken Brown Rubber Stamps, lightning by Stamp Oasis, and spark plug by Gumbo Graphics.*

Making the Transfer Paper for Stamping

1. Stack about ten sheets of white typing paper (avoid nonerasable) or a paper type and size suitable to your project. The stack also serves as a padded surface on which to stamp. The transfer ink pads are available from Comotion stamp company as "Stamp 'N' Iron."

2. Press the stamp onto a transfer ink pad several times until you achieve good coverage. Close the stamp pad cover to prevent drying out the ink. Press the stamp onto the first sheet of the paper stack.

3. Repeat the process until you have a number of good clear impressions. Make more than you think you'll need before changing to a new stamp. Nothing is more frustrating than running out of an image during the ironing process. If you are alternating several stamps, place the stamp not in use face down on wet paper towels in a Styrofoam tray to keep the ink from hardening. Before using the stamp again, blot away excess water so you don't dilute the ink in the stamp pad.

4. Allow the stamped paper to dry (10 minutes or longer). While you are waiting, wash the ink off your stamps. Also, check your transfer papers closely for any unwanted ink marks or dirty finger smudges. If they occur on the outside of the image, cut away those sections of paper. If they are inside your image, paint over them with a white-out fluid. Two coats with thorough drying in between will prevent the color from bleeding through.

Ironing the Transfer Paper to Fabric

The following procedure is to be used for ironing all forms of the transfer dyes (inks, crayons, paint, etc.) to fabric. As the paper size and dye coating may vary (ex. stamping is a thin dye layer, painting a thicker layer), adjust your heat transfer time accordingly. Iron in a well-ventilated room; respirator recommended.

SPECIALTY STAMPS
Wheel Stamps and Texture Cubes

Most commercial stamps are composed of a chunk of wood with a rubber image attached. Two other types of stamps are available for use with dye transfer inks: wheel stamps and texture cubes.

Like small tires, wheel stamps roll a band of pattern across the fabric (Fig. 8-1). The width and length of the printed band depends on the wheel's dimensions. The stamping wheels I prefer are ½" to 1" wide and will deposit about 7" of strong color before making a second, less inked, lighter rotation (see 8-6).

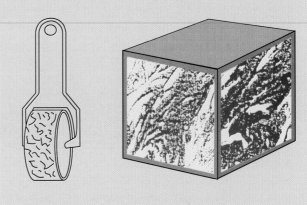

Fig. 8-1 Wheel stamp and texture cube

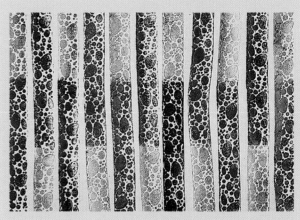

8-6 Although most wheel stamps work best with the dye transfer inks, those that have large, strongly-defined patterns can be used with fabric paints. Clearsnap's "droplets" wheel stamp, worked well with paints to show how the first rotation applies a heavy layer of color before making a lighter less inked rotation.

Wheel stamps are available in numerous images, border prints, and—best of all—textures. Wheels and handles are often sold separately, so that purchasing many wheels and only a few handles will save money. The wheels simply snap onto the handles.

Using the wheel with transfer inks is easy. Remove a sheet of typing paper from the stack and place it on a section of newspaper that has no lumps or creases. Ink the wheel by rolling it on the ink pad while applying light pressure. Be sure it is inked around its total circumference. Position the wheel near, but not on, one edge of the typing paper. Keep the wheel flat on the surface and push or pull the wheel from one edge of the paper to the opposite edge without stopping. You need not roll in orderly straight lines; the band can curve, or it can crisscross another band to form a checkerboard pattern, a figure eight, or a triangle. Colors can be overlapped on the paper to create new tones, be cut out and separated, or form a background for solid image stamps (see 8-7).

Instead of being round like a wheel stamp, a texture cube resembles a child's big wooden block. It is actually three stamps in one, with a different rubber image on three of its six sides. When stamped over each other, the three sides/images combine to produce an overall texture. For example, to create a marbled pattern, side A is inked with yellow and stamped across the fabric with a loose registration.

Side B is then inked with pink and stamped directly over pattern A. Finally, a dark purple is used on side C and stamped over the A and B patterns. The result is a multicolored, marble-like texture that has a sense of depth (Fig. 8-2). Different textures are available: knotty wood, fibrous paper, a plaid, confetti, and so forth. Of course, each side of the cube may be used alone or mixed with other images.

As the cube is fairly large, you may need to bring the pad to the stamp and tap on the color. Or you can purchase a large sized, inkless pad and fill it yourself with a refill bottle. Always clean the cube's surfaces immediately after printing so paint doesn't dry in the delicate details and become difficult to remove.

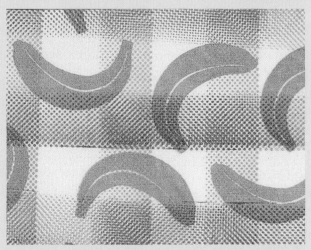

8-7 When a wheel stamp texture appears over and then under a solid image stamp, a sense of depth is created. *Copyrighted images: "screen fade" rollagraph wheel stamp by Clearsnap, Inc. and the banana shape by Hampton Art Stamps, Inc.*

Fig. 8-2 When these three sides are inked with different colors and stamped over one another, a marble texture results. *Texture cube by Stampendous Inc.*

1. Cover your support surface (ironing board, cardboard) with clean paper to protect it from dye bleed through. Do not use newspaper as the heat may transfer the black ink to your cloth. Place the fabric right side up on the surface and position the transfer paper face down onto the fabric. Remember that all images will be reversed after transfer.

2. Set the iron to a cotton or hot setting. Do not use steam, and make sure no moisture remains in the iron. Cover the fabric and transfer paper with a sheet of tissue paper which will help to protect the fabric from the high heat and to hold the transfer paper in place. Iron over each section of the transfer paper design for 15 to 40 seconds, or whatever your test samples indicated. Use a gentle pressure, and keep the iron moving slightly to avoid imprinting the steam holes. Make sure the hot center area of the iron contacts all sections of the transfer paper equally. Resist returning to an already ironed section, as the paper will have shifted and a blurred image will result.

   Although the manufacturer's instructions recommend certain times, the actual time required for a good transfer may vary. Your iron, the ironing board cover (cotton covers may not get as hot as metallic looking ones), the paper type, the fabric density, the thickness of collaged papers, and how you time the seconds, may all affect dye transfer. Always do test strips first. Only you can determine the exact time needed to develop the color and transfer the image. To check on the color progress, lift a corner of the transfer paper while the iron holds most of the paper firmly. Do not allow the transfer paper to shift. If you stop the process as soon as the desired color is achieved, you may be able to use the paper several times.

3. Remove the tissue paper and the used transfer paper. Discard the tissue paper and the protective paper under the fabric, which may be contaminated with dye. If you do a second transfer, next to the first, be sure to cover the first one with clean

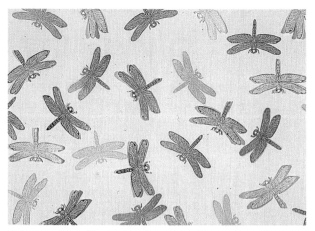

8-8 A variety of colors and two-toned images can be made by overlaying colors. In this fabric, a light value dragonfly was printed on the fabric from a used paper transfer. Then a second, unused dragonfly image was cut out and registered directly over the first. *The dragonfly is a copyrighted image of All Night Media.*

paper to protect it from the iron's heat. The second and third transfer will be lighter but can be used as a base color for color overlays (see 8-8).

WAX TRANSFER CRAYONS

Everybody loves a new box of crayons. Although transfer crayons don't come in 100 shades to entice us, Binney and Smith do manufacture eight colors that can be overlaid on the transfer paper for additional color blends.

Transfer crayons work exactly as your childhood crayons, so feel free to try anything on the paper: overlay many colors, cut or tear out shapes from patterned sheets, make rubbings (lace, wood, nets), scribble over masked out areas, and collage images from a coloring book.

Wax transfer crayons can also be melted to create designs. Cut or shave the crayon into small slivers, and sandwich the pieces between two sheets of paper. Iron over the layers, which will melt the color to the paper and produce two mirror images for transfer.

Unlike the inks used for stamping, crayons deposit a heavy layer of waxy color

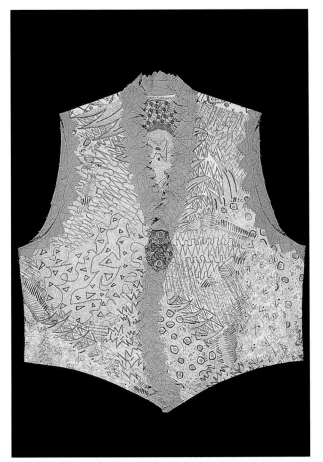

on the paper. So be sure to check your images for chunks of crayon, which can be removed with the sticky side of masking tape. If left intact, these bits of color could spread into blobs when your design is heated. Even worse, they could drop onto your ironing board and suddenly become part of your favorite white blouse.

TRANSFER MARKER PENS

Sulky® Iron-On pens are the perfect tools for transferring images where precision is important (line drawings, facial features, delicate details). And if you like to work with a pen, you'll love the convenience and flexibility of these markers. One of my favorite uses is for children's drawings. You can let the child work directly on paper with the eight different colors of transfer pens and then iron the finished work onto the fabric. Or you can collaborate. Let the child do the line drawing in

8-9 Have fun and be spontaneous when working with wax transfer crayons. Vest and polymer clay pin by Carolyn Dahl.

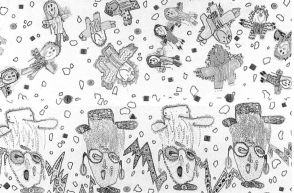

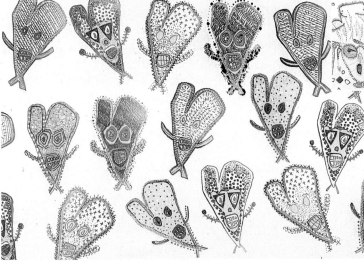

8-10 Collaboration with children. The line drawings above were created by five-year-old Kate Sharp (top) and seven-year-old Brett Boser (bottom) and transferred to fabric with Sulky® Iron-On pens. The colors and patterns were added later by the author with regular textile markers.

8-11 After my eye surgery, my nephew, Brett Boser, sent me this line drawing of an "angry heart" complete with shocked eyes and screaming mouth. Somehow he had captured in a child's way, the fear, the anger, the pain, and the love that surrounded me during the experience. So I reproduced his heart image on paper, added color and pattern with the Sulky® pens, and transferred the hearts to fabric. Then I divided it in two. Now, like two halves of one heart, we each have a piece of cloth that represents our shared experience and collaboration.

8-12 The mad hatter stamp was enlarged on the photo-copy machine and transferred to the fabric with Sulky® Iron-On pens. Marvy and FabricMate textile markers were used to correct transfer lines and to add color to stamped images and quilt labels. *Copyrighted stamp images: mad hatter, cup and saucer, teapot by Inkadinkado, Inc.; birth-day cake set, jumbo surprise bag by Stampendous, Inc.; pen by Posh Impressions; fortune cookie, pear by Rubber Stampede; cosmos, checkerboard frame by All Night Media; Plexiglas signature stamp by Pelle's; water/leaves by Hampton Art Stamps, Inc.*

A second way to use the Sulky® Iron-On pens is to transfer images that have been enlarged on the photocopy machine. For instance, I wanted to use some of the stamped images from Inkadinkado's Alice In Wonder-land stamp set. However, I needed a larger size than the stamp provided for my project. By enlarging the stamped image on a photo-copy machine, and then tracing over the lines of the photocopy with the transfer pens, I was able to reproduce the larger size image on my fabric (the image will be reversed).

Remember though, that all images on commercial stamps are copyrighted. You may use the images for your personal hand-stamping use. However, if you plan to reproduce or enlarge the stamp images for commercial purposes, you must secure the suppliers' permission by writing them.

Dye-Saturated Paper Sheets

Design-Dye™ sheets are 8" x 10" paper sheets that have been coated with the heat-transfer dyes. Eight different colors of the dye-saturated sheets are available. Although they can be cut up into shapes and ironed directly onto the fabric, I prefer to use their nice even surfaces to coat other objects such as fresh leaves or photocopies of photographs, and then transfer these images to the fabric.

The sheets are covered with a heavy layer of dye, so handle and store the sheets with care. As with the crayon-colored papers, you don't want the papers to rub against or drop specks of color on other surfaces.

The manufacturer of Design-Dye™ sheets also sells a spray solution called Fabric-Prep for those of you who love cotton and don't want to use synthetic fabrics. Spraying your washed cotton, or blends with a high percent-age of cotton, will prepare the fabric chemi-cally to accept the dye sheets and to increase color retention.

Leaf Transfer

1. Select a fresh leaf that is no larger than your iron plate. Avoid thick, fleshy, or juice (milk) producing leaves. Iron

one or more transfer pen colors, iron the work to the fabric, and then you embellish it with regular textile markers (see 8-10, 8-11, page 93).

Although the transfer marker pen colors are permanent, and I often create a finished project with them on the paper, regular textile markers do offer a few more color options when coloring directly on the fabric. Also the different application tips (fine line, broad, chisel, and brush) make it easy to match the tip size to the shape space. Some brands even have a nib on one end and a brush on the other, or a light color on one end and a darker value on the other.

Test all textile markers first on scrap fabric to get a feel for how far the color will bleed and to match colors. Once you feel comfort-able with the different markers, you can color in a transferred drawing, correct gaps in lines that didn't transfer properly, enhance hand-stamped labels, or sign your work (see 8-12). Always follow the manufacturers' instructions if the textile marker colors need to be heat-set.

94

the fresh leaf between paper to remove the moisture and flatten the surface somewhat. The leaf should be relatively dry.

2. Lay the leaf, vein side up, on a piece of paper. Cover the leaf with a rectangle of the Design-Dye paper, colored side down,

and iron with pressure for about 35–40 seconds. The color will now have transferred from the paper to the leaf's surface.

3. Place the leaf on the fabric coated side down, cover with tissue paper, and iron again to transfer the color from the leaf to the fabric (approximately 20–30 seconds).

8-13 *Eye Veils* by Carolyn Dahl. Background fabric sponge printed, circles stamped with marble texture cube by Stampendous, photo transfer with Design-Dye sheets and Deka IronOn paint. Photo by Maria Davila.

When you remove the leaf, you will have a leaf print, complete with veins. If you plan to use the same leaf the next day, place it in a book to keep it flat. The technique can also be done with flowers, ferns, feathers, and other natural objects.

Photograph Transfer

1. Choose a photograph that has a strong value contrast (definite dark and light areas) and clear sharp details. Select several different settings on the photocopy machine and run copies. Each machine will give different results. Sometimes a too dark copy will cause the dye paper and photocopy to stick together. But if the copy is too light, the details of the photograph may not transfer. Try different settings and machines.

2. Lay down a piece of cardboard covered in newsprint. Sometimes the soft surface of an ironing board has too much give to transfer all the nuances of a photograph, so the cardboard gives a harder, more even surface. Lay the photocopied photograph face up and cover with a sheet of Design-Dye™ paper cut to size, face down. Cover with tissue paper, and iron with a hot dry iron for a count of about 20–30. Allow to cool slightly before pulling apart slowly. The color from the sheet will have adhered to the toner in the photocopy. The deep blue dye sheets are especially nice to use as they resemble blueprinted images when finished.

3. Cut away any background of the dye-coated photocopy you do not want to print. The image can also be cut into various interesting shapes before transfer. Lay the photocopy face down on the cloth. Cover with tissue paper and iron to transfer. If you make a second transfer, be sure to change all the protective papers which might be contaminated with some of the dye.

USED INDUSTRIAL DYE SHEETS

Many textile printing companies recycle their used heat transfer papers. If you watch closely, you can find these papers made into notepads, wrapping paper, notebook paper, and store bags. Although they have been used already, the papers still have enough residual dye to deposit a pattern on your fabric.

It's not always easy to tell if the paper you're considering is a dye sheet or not. But look for paper that has one shiny side, almost glazed looking, and one dull matte side. The colors will have a mellow, toned-down quality, as the most vibrant dye has already been removed during printing. It also doesn't feel like a strong, expensive paper, which is probably why my best sources are discount stores. And the last hint that it may be what you're looking for, is that the pattern looks like something you would see on fabric.

Of course there is no way to know how your paper will print until you test it with a hot iron. Because the heaviest layer of dye is gone, you will need to increase your transfer time considerably. Always do a test swatch first. Each pattern will transfer differently. Some papers give wonderful pastel tones; others transfer only sections of the design; and still others produce colors that are so vibrant you'd think it was the first printing.

READY-TO-USE TRANSFER PAINT

You can also paint your own dye sheets with Deka® IronOn transfer paint. The set comes in six ready-to-use colors that can be thinned with water. As you prepare the transfer sheet yourself, you can mix custom colors, dilute or intensify the color values, scrape into the paint for texture, or paint a complete picture for transfer to fabric.

Before painting, shake each bottle well. Paint your design on a nonabsorbent sheet of paper that won't wrinkle from the moisture or you'll get a blotchy transfer. For most purposes, apply a smooth, medium thick layer, which will give at least two transfers.

The more paint applied to the paper, the greater the number of usable transfers.

When I'm working with large areas of color, or photocopied images, I always apply at least two coats of paint. I paint on one layer, let it dry, and apply another to get an even transfer. All patterns will be reversed when ironed on, so letters and numbers must be painted backwards to print correctly. Let the painted paper dry completely before transferring to fabric.

Besides painting, the transfer paint can be used for sponging, rolling, printing, and stamping. If you are unable to find the transfer ink stamp pads, the Deka® IronOn paint can be substituted. Either apply the paint directly to the stamp with a foam brush, or pour it onto a homemade stamp pad that can be washed after use (piece of wet felt, foam, or several layers of Pellon in a plastic tray) (see 8-14).

POWDERED DISPERSED DYES

If you don't mind mixing your own colors, powdered dispersed dyes called PROsperse dyes are available from PRO Chemical and Dye. As the powder is added to water, the colors will be very liquid. A thickener may be needed to give the viscosity necessary for painting or printing applications. If you plan to use transfer dyes in large quantities and want a greater color selection, mixing your own dyes from the powders will be more economical.

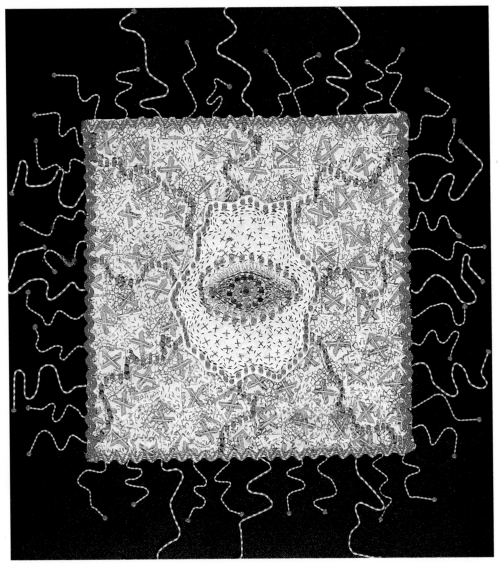

8-14 *The Eye in I* by Carolyn Dahl. Deka IronOn paints were used for stamped designs and painted eye. *"X" from an alphabet stamp set by Ranger Industries.*

Chapter 9

SELF-DESIGNED STAMPS

Any object can be a stamp if it can be coated with color and pressed onto fabric. When we made our first refrigerator art by dipping our hands into red tempera paint and pressing them to paper, we were using our hands as stamps. A search around the yard, the garage, or through kitchen utensils will quickly turn up other objects that can be used as stamps. However, if you have a specific image in mind, you will want to create your own.

Depending on your design, there are several ways to proceed. If your design has many fine details, and isn't too large, the best choice may be sending your drawing to a commercial company to be made into a rubber stamp for you (California Rubber Stamp Co.). However, if your design calls for bold, simple shapes, it's easy to make your own stamps from sheet or block materials (see 9-3, page 100). Sheet materials are thin (flexible printing plates, sheet foam, polystyrene plates) and can be cut into shapes and glued to a flat support to create the stamp. Block materials are thicker (erasers, rubber blocks), and are carved to remove the sections of the design you don't want to print. Both materials accept

9-1 Susan Farm-Heumann used copyright free images from a Dover book, *African Designs from Traditional Sources* by Geoffrey Williams, to create her stamps for this vest. Adding a frog shape from Pelle's African image collection, she completed her theme with ethnic-inspired commercial fabric and bone buttons. Versatex fabric paint on cotton.

fabric paint or thickened dyes well when applied with a small sponge or brush.

No matter how the stamp is made, the first print will always surprise you. Even though I've planned every detail of the image, spent time carving and building it, I've learned that I don't really know my own stamp until I print it.

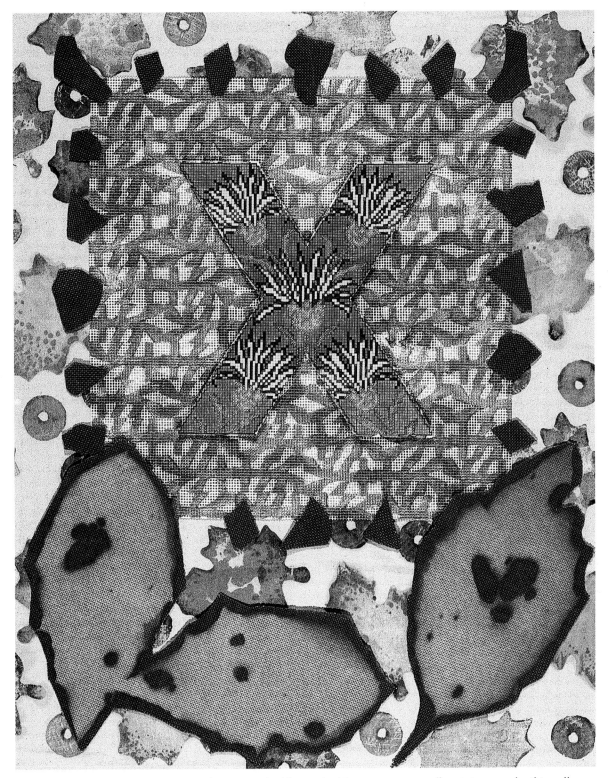

9-2 A carved eraser stamp was used to create the blue and white pattern on needlepoint canvas for this collage. By Carolyn Dahl.

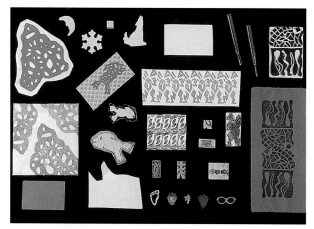

9-3 Stamp making materials. Starting at left, going down in loosely defined rows. Row 1: Turquoise sheet foam cut into lace-like design, mounted on foam board, and stamped on fabric with gold paint. Row 2: Wooden cut-outs; fish stamp cut from flexible printing plate, mounted on foam board and stamped on patterned fabric. Sample at bottom shows a corner of the white protective paper removed to reveal the adhesive-covered gray plate material. Row 3: White rubber block before carving; fabric stamped with a carved figure block; carved eraser stamps and fabric sample; school erasers shapes for stamping. Row 4: Wood carving tools, carved rubber block, and printed fabric.

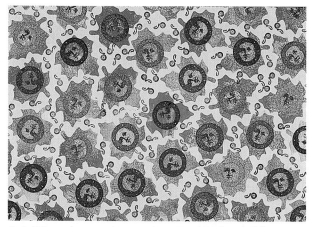

9-4 When the wood stamp is not covered with felt, which would absorb and hold more paint, the stamp applies a thin coat of color. Thus commercial stamps can be printed over the first image without getting a heavy paint buildup. *Copyrighted stamp images: Moon by Rubber Stampede, and pocket watch by Inkadinkado. Opaque and pearlized fabric paint by Createx, and textile markers by Marvy.*

DESIGNING YOUR STAMP

Decide if the stamp will be a single unit placed randomly across the fabric, or a unit that touches and interlocks with another to form a repetitive pattern. If used as a random, single unit, any design or image will work. If, however, you want stamp images to form an interactive pattern that changes depending on how the stamp is rotated, you must consider the stamp's outline. For example, if you carved a circle in an eraser, it doesn't matter if you rotate the eraser to the left or to the right, or turn it upside down. The design will always look like one circle next to another circle. But a stamp with an interesting outline, with edges that protrude and recede, makes new shapes every time it rotates and connects to another.

To test one of your designs, make eight exact squares on a sheet of graph paper. Trace your design onto each square and cut the squares apart. Or you can photocopy your design unit repeatedly, cut out the units, and arrange them into different combinations (see Patterns 1-4). Once you have a pattern you like, glue the paper units into place for reference, and begin making your stamp. (Cut the design in reverse so the final print will be the same as the original drawing.)

Stamp Materials

FLEXIBLE PRINTING PLATE: Flexible printing plate is a smooth, durable vinyl-like material, about $1/16$" thick, that can be cut with scissors or an X-ACTO knife. It is sold in sheets, approximately 9 x 12", and may also be called Sure Stamp or Speedball printing plate. The stamp is made by cutting the image out of the sheet and attaching it with glue stick to a support, such as foam board, cardboard, Plexiglas, or wood. If the support is trimmed to match the contour of the image, about $1/4$" to $1/2$" from the edge, exact placement on the fabric is easier.

Some brands of the printing plate come with a self-adhesive backing. After tracing your design on the vinyl side (not the paper side) and cutting out the image, the protective paper layer over the adhesive is peeled away

UNIT A

Side 1

Side 4   Side 2

Side 3

UNIT A STAMP

Stamp Prints in Reverse

UNIT B

Side 1

Side 4   Side 2

Side 3

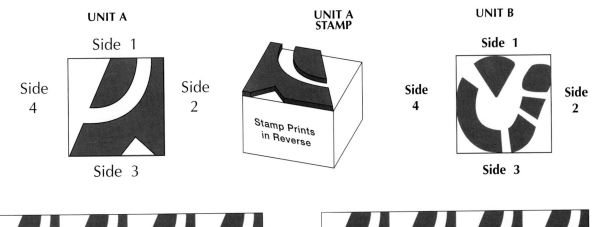

Pattern 1

Pattern 2

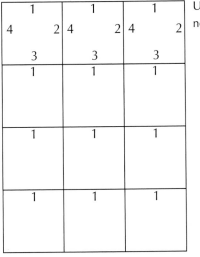

1		1		1	
4	2	4	2	4	2
	3		3		3
1		1		1	
1		1		1	
1		1		1	

Unit A repeated with no rotations.

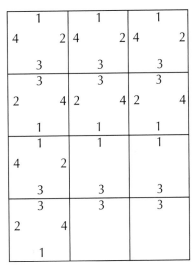

	1		1		1	
4		2	4	2	4	2
	3		3		3	
	3		3		3	
2		4	2	4	2	4
	1		1		1	
	1		1		1	
4		2				
	3		3		3	
	3		3		3	
2		4				
	1					

Unit A repeated across row.

Unit A rotated upside down and repeated across row.

PATTERNS 1–4   Pattern making possibilities of stamped designs. The units, A & B, and four patterns.

and the image attached easily to the support.

If you have a problem with the background area printing, you may need to raise the image. Cut an identical shape from the printing plate and attach it onto the one already on your support. The additional layer should give enough depth to keep your background from making contact with the fabric. If not, try stamping on a harder surface.

After stamping, remove the colorant from your design by wiping it with a wet sponge and blotting the stamp repeatedly on paper towels. A soft brush can be used to gently remove color caught in details. Unless your support material is waterproof, do not place the stamp under running water to clean it. Cardboard and paper-covered foam board will deteriorate and warp.

Pattern 3

Unit A repeated with a rotation every other print.

	3			1			3			1	
2		4	4		2	2		4	4		2
	1			3			1			3	
	1			3			1			3	
4		2	2		4	4		2	2		4
	3			1			3			1	
	3			1			3			1	
2		4	4		2						
	1			3							
				3			1			1	
4		2	2		4						
	3			1							

Pattern 4

Unit A alternated with a new unit B. Many additional designs are possible when a new unit is added.

	1			1			1			1	
4	Ⓐ	2	4	Ⓑ	2	4	Ⓐ	2	4	Ⓑ	2
	3			3			3			3	
	1			1							
4	Ⓑ	2	4	Ⓐ	2						
	3			3							
	1										
4	Ⓐ	2									
	3										
	1										
4	Ⓑ	2									
	3										

Flexible printing plate can also be used to create your own wheel stamps. Cut the pieces of your design out of the plate and adhere them to a hard wooden roller.

SHEET FOAM: Usually found in craft stores, these soft foam sheets are fluffier and a little thicker than the flexible printing plates. They can be purchased in colors and cut with a scissors. When selecting sheets, choose those that are free of dents, air bubble holes, and scratches which will print. The foam sheets can also be layered on a support for greater printing depth. A brand called "sticky foam" comes with a self-adhesive backing. When printed, the image has a slightly granular texture that gives a beautiful quality to bold shapes. Following printing, the foam stamp should be cleaned very gently with a wet sponge to prevent marring the spongy surface.

A similar type of sheet foam is the firmer polystyrene foam ("polyprint," "polystyrene printing plates"), which resembles the plastic used in meat trays or take-out food containers. These white foam sheets are extremely easy to cut into shapes, but have an additional advantage. Hard objects can be pressed into the surface of the polystyrene plate and the impression will remain. It is especially useful for making reverse prints of rubber stamps. Also, you can draw into the surface with a ballpoint pen to create a print where the lines are white.

ERASERS: Eraser stamping is often equated with children's projects and dismissed as too simple to warrant exploration. But complexity of a tool is not important; what is important is the character of the tool's mark. Each material has an individual imprint that cannot be duplicated exactly by another material. If an

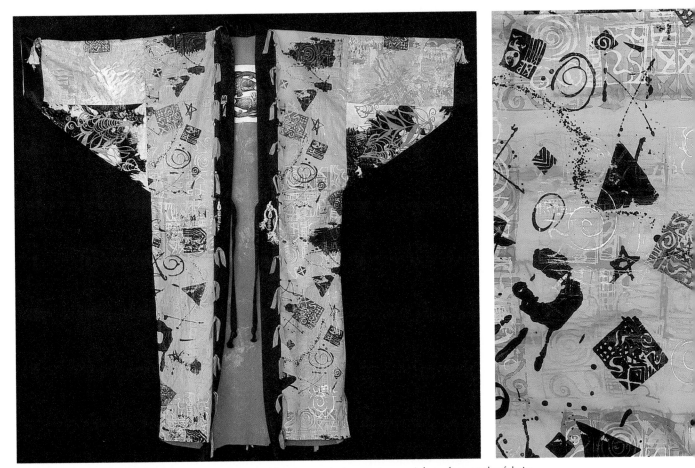

9-5 Mixing eraser stamps with other techniques gives a rich surface to the fabric.
9-6 *Japanese Raincoat* by Jane Dunnewold and Renita Kuhn. Dyes, Deka silk paints, puff ink, foil, and textile inks.

eraser gives an impression that works with your concept, then it is the right tool to use, simple or not (see 9-2, page 99).

I like the humble art gum erasers. They have an uncomplicated, almost primitive charm. Maybe they're not as durable as other erasers, but they are easy to find in grocery or drug stores, and easy to carve. Their surface is small, soft, and tender, forcing me to simplify. When the stamp and I have spent many months together, and its edges get too ragged to print well, I don't abandon it. I simply trim away the bad sections, glue two or three erasers together, and create a new printing block out of their combined images. Finally, when they are beyond hope, I return them to their modest beginnings as functioning art erasers. Within minutes, I've carved a whole new batch of replacements and I'm ready to stamp again.

However, if you want a larger image area, or prefer a harder stamp that lasts for years, consider these erasers: Magicrub, Mars Staedtler Grand, Nasco, Pink Pearl, E. F. Eberhard Faber Plastic Race, RubKleen®, and Pedigree® by Empire.

Carving Erasers

1. Prepare a simple design on paper first. Most erasers have a crumbly consistency and a small carving surface area, so keep the design elements to a minimum.

2. Trace the drawing onto the eraser. Try not to change your mind as the former pencil lines will make indentations in the eraser. Once you ink the surface and press it on the fabric, they will reappear as ghost lines in your design.

3. Using an X-ACTO knife, cut away all areas you do not want to print. Insert the knife and cut straight down, or angle away from the design element. Do not undercut.

4. Apply the color with a foam brush or a small cosmetic sponge. Stiff bristled brushes will sometimes scratch the surface of soft erasers. After printing, clean the

erasers carefully with your fingers and water. Kind hearted cleaning is the secret to extending the life of your eraser stamps.

RUBBER BLOCKS: Sold under various names (Soft-Kut, Softoleum, Safety-Kut, Safe N' E-Z Cut, and Soft Cut), these rubber-like white blocks are the perfect substitute for the hard-to-cut linoleum blocks often used in fabric printing. They can be purchased in small ready-to-carve blocks (4" x 6", 6" x 12", etc.) or in larger sizes (up to 18" x 26"), which can be cut to size. Simply score the surface by pulling a knife along a line, bend the block at that line, and tear the two pieces apart. The depth of most blocks is $1/4$" or $3/8$". The thicker blocks can be carved on both sides, but I recommend carving only one side as the cuts need to be deeper for fabric printing than for paper printing.

Transferring Design to Block

You can draw on the design, use tracing paper, or easiest of all, transfer a photocopy following this procedure:

1. Start with a high contrast, black-and-white image or drawing that you want to transfer to the block. Dover books provide some good copyright-free shapes and patterns for generating ideas.

2. Photocopy the image, enlarging or reducing to fit the block. Make copies on several machines and note which was used on the backside of your copy. Some machines will give good transfers and others won't.

3. Lay the photocopy, image side down, onto your rubber block. Cover both with an old sheet or piece of muslin to act as a pressing cloth.

4. Set your iron to a cotton setting. Press down on the cloth for a count of five with the hot iron. This will cause the toner to stick onto the block so the paper won't shift around as much. Then move the iron

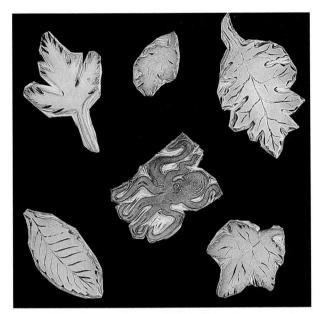

9-7 Rubber block stamps carved by Susan Farm-Heumann.

block, however, you will know what feels the most comfortable to you (see 9-7).

Whatever method you use, work slowly, carefully, and safely to avoid cutting yourself. Choose a quiet, calm time of the day so you can focus and guide the tools smoothly. Coffee addicts like myself should limit their java intake on carving day, as a sure, steady hand is a necessity. To help prevent accidents, always hold the block firmly. The rubbery composition of the material sticks slightly to the work surface, which helps prevent slipping or skidding when carving pressure is applied. However, always keep the non-carving hand well away from the moving tool's path. Wherever possible, work from the interior of the design out to the edge. That way, if you slip, your tool will go off the edge and not into your design or your hand.

in small circles for about 10 seconds or count slowly to 10.

5. Peel back a corner of the photocopy to see if the image has transferred. It should be almost as dark on the block as it was on the paper. If the image looks fuzzy, iron a little longer.

6. When the image has transferred, peel off the paper while it is still warm. The photocopy can often be used 2–3 times more, so save it. You can now follow the image, which is in reverse, to carve your block.

Carving the Block

1. Lay the block on a work surface that you do not mind nicking if your cutting tool slips. Covering tables with a piece of strong cardboard or masonite will help if no other support is available.

2. Carve out the design with standard linoleum cutters or wood carving tools. I prefer to start with a small V-shaped liner tool and outline the design areas I want to keep. Then I switch to a larger U-shaped gouge to remove the background areas I don't want to print. After carving your first

3. After completing the carving, remove all flakes and chunks of rubber that may be caught in the grooves and depressions. Now test your design on a sample piece of fabric. Dab on your color with a sponge or brush and stamp onto fabric. Because the block is thick, you will need to press harder, or rub the backside of the block with your hand, or even pound gently on the block to transfer the color to the fabric. Do not rock or bounce the block, however. Lift the block off the fabric to check the test print. If background areas have printed, additional carving may be necessary to lower those sections.

4. Clean the block after printing by holding it under water and rubbing the paint off with your fingers, or a soft sponge or brush. Soap may be used. Occasionally, after repeated printings with fabric paints, the block continues to feel sticky after washing. Fingernail polish remover can be used to remove some, but not all, paint brands from the rubber surface.

Chapter
10

DESTRUCTION PATTERNS

*I*f there is a demon in the mythology of dyeing, it would be bleach. A destroyer, it attacks the dye, breaking apart its chemical bonds, and forcing the fabric to release the color. It takes only a few minutes for a rich black fabric to turn brown, then tan, and finally the color of bones.

While bleach destroys the color, it can also be harsh to the fabric. The chemicals that remove the color can seriously weaken the cloth's fibers if careful and correct procedures are not used. Unfortunately, the fiber degradation isn't always apparent immediately.

DISCHARGE/BLEACH PATTERNS

I remember a dark gray, cotton fabric that I discharged to a dusty pink pattern. I had applied the bleach with a brush in a loose, free-form design. As a brush leaves less bleach on the fabric than many other application methods, I wasn't too worried about damage. However, I still checked my fabric for weak areas by holding it up to the light to detect thin spots, and then tugging in both directions on any suspicious looking areas. Thus I was pretty surprised when the second machine washing produced holes in exactly the same shapes as some of the design elements. Apparently, I had made two mistakes. My bleach was too concentrated for the delicate, lightweight cotton, and I had failed to neutralize the fabric properly. The machine's agitation had finally caused the weakened areas to drop entirely out of the fabric.

If bleaching requires such risk, why would anyone want to discharge fabric? Well, maybe you won't. You must be totally entranced and intrigued with the results.

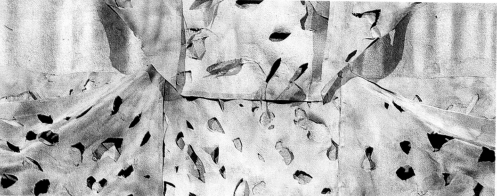

10-1 *Nuclear Forest #3* (facing page) and detail (above), by Carolyn Dahl.
Silk bleach, multiple dye applications, burning, and slashing were used to achieve the destruction theme. Photograph by Michael McCormick.

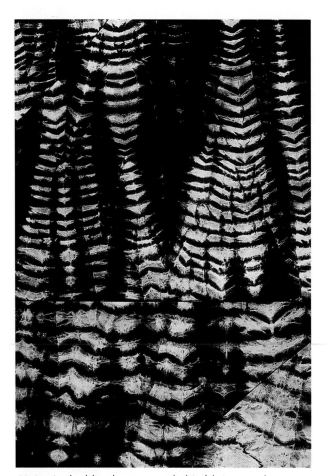

10-2 As the bleach progressed, this fabric turned many wonderful shades of brown before arriving at the warm tan color. If I had wanted to stop the action and preserve the brown tones, I could have moved the fabric quickly to the neutralizer.

10-3 Different color values can be achieved by varying the concentration of bleach and techniques. Some of the darker pink areas were discharged with a weak bleach solution and the lightest pinks with a strong bleach solution.

Colors that have been bleached always have an off-beat tonal range to me. In most fabric design techniques, color is added (or charged) onto the white fabric. But in bleaching, you begin with a commercially or hand-dyed colored fabric and remove (or discharge, subtract) the color. The color that is left behind always has a peculiar quality. It's not a new color, but one that has disappeared against its will. What remains is like a shadow, or ghost, of a former color.

I've often tried to reproduce a bleached color with my dyes. Although I can come near, my mixture never "feels" like the color. It never has that disquieting emotional tone. Sure, it's a faded yellow, but it is not the yellow color of the sky before a tornado that the bleach leaves behind.

Besides its strange colors, some of the evocative power of discharged fabric comes from the destructive process itself—the fabric's brush with danger. The fabric always carries a trace of the chemical assault in its pattern, and for some purposes and images, I find that a most appropriate characteristic.

When I did my series of "Nuclear Forest" silk panels, I wanted to make a statement about destroying the environment. I could think of no textile process other than discharging that could portray a destructive force, and no fabric more precious than silk to represent our beautiful, fragile earth. If I had not been able to chemically attack the silk with bleach, to burn it with fire, and to slash its surface, I would not have been able to convey the statement I wanted to make. Even though the silk

10-4 The fabric was compressed and bound before being painted with bleach.

works may still look very beautiful in a photo, when the viewer stands next to their seven-foot-high presence, you can feel the assault that took place on their surfaces.

Discharging requires courage. The dyer must risk destroying the cloth to make the fabric become something else. But it also requires diligence. I may let the bleach lead, but I do everything I can to minimize and prevent damage to the fiber. With proper precautions, you can control the demon and produce fabrics with haunting colors and patterns.

1. Always test a swatch of the fabric to be discharged and keep records of the results.

2. Match the fiber to the correct bleaching agent.

3. Use the smallest amount of bleach possible to achieve the effects.

4. Choose a strong fabric instead of delicate, lightweight cloth until you have more experience with the bleaching process.

5. Allow the fabric to contact the bleach the least amount of time.

6. Use a neutralizer after bleaching to stop the chemical action.

7. Wash the fabric promptly and thoroughly to remove all traces of the bleach.

Discharge Agent

The discharge agent we will use in this chapter is the familiar chlorine bleach (sodium hypochlorite, or Chlorox, Purex). An easy-to-use liquid, chlorine has been around since 1787 when Carl Wilhelm Scheele recognized its color removing properties.[1] It can discharge cotton, viscose rayon, and linen, but will damage protein fibers such as silk and wool. Thiourea dioxide (also known as Spectralite) and Formosul (use with caution) can be used on protein fibers. If in doubt as to which discharge agent to use, consult your dye supplier who can direct you to the proper bleach for your fiber.

Sodium alginate or monagum (a starch) can be used to thicken the bleach solution for stamping and printing procedures. The thickened pastes will only last 2–3 hours, however, as the bleach breaks down the binders rather quickly. So mix up only as much discharge paste as you can use in one session.

Even though chlorine bleach is a common household laundry bleach, safety precautions are necessary because we are using the product in ways the manufacturer never intended. Usually bleach is diluted with a large amount of water and agitated in a closed machine. With discharge patterning, however, the bleach solution is highly concentrated and applied by hand methods, which increase your exposure to its corrosive effects.

• Work outside or in a well ventilated area

10-5 Black fabric gives the most dramatic results. One never knows what colors were used to achieve the rich black and thus what colors will appear.

such as an open garage. Do not inhale the fumes, and always wear a respirator with an organic vapor filter.

• Do not mix the bleach with other substances or with other bleaching agents as harmful or irritating gases or vapors could result. Use plastic or glass containers instead of metal.

• Protect your skin by wearing long-sleeve shirts, long pants, and kitchen (not surgical) rubber gloves. Always protect your precious eyes with chemical splash goggles, safety goggles, or at the very least eye glasses. Execute all techniques with the fewest splashes or spatters possible.

• Read all of the manufacturer's precautions and instructions before beginning; then follow them. Keep bleach out of the reach of children and always close and cap the container immediately after use.

The Neutralizer

To stop the chemical action of the bleach, the fabric must be soaked in a neutralizing solution. If you skip the neutralizer and just wash the fabric, you aren't halting the bleaching action immediately. The bleach will become diluted and less powerful in the wash water, but until it is completely removed from the fabric, or neutralized, it will continue acting on the cloth even when dry. We may not need to worry about bleach residue in our laundry as most clothing is replaced within several years. Why jeopardize the longevity of your artwork however, when such a simple step can prevent damage.

Regular household white vinegar is often used as a neutralizer, but a more reliable substance is sodium bisulfite, or Anti-Chlor (available from PRO Chemical and Dye). It comes as a powder, which keeps one year if covered and stored in a dark place. Once mixed with water, the unused solution will keep for several weeks if it is kept cool and covered. After use, however, it cannot be reused and must be discarded.

The recipe for sodium bisulfite is 1 tablespoon per 1 quart of water. For Anti-Chlor:

approximately 1 level teaspoon Anti-Chlor per pound of fabric (approximately 1–2 yards of light to medium weight fabric) in $2^1/2$ gallons of hot water (110°F). Submerge the discharged and rinsed fabric in the neutralizer. Agitate for about five minutes and rinse well.

Making Fabric Test Samples

Not all fabrics can be bleached successfully. Some are too delicate and fragile, have finishes that resist the bleach, or contain dyes that will not discharge (especially expensive fabrics). Although approximately 60 to 70 percent of industrial dyes now in use will discharge to some degree, every so often you will encounter one that refuses to release its color to chlorine bleach. After all, fabric manufacturers spend a great deal of time and money developing colors that "won't fade in the wash."

In general, sturdy cottons and dark colors, especially black, will give the most dramatic results. As deep toned colors are usually composed of others, you never know exactly what color will appear in the bleached areas. Blacks usually yield brown, tan, yellow, or gray-white, but sometimes they'll surprise you with wonderful shades of pink and peach.

So before investing in a lot of fabric that may not discharge, purchase $1/8$ of a yard of those colors you are considering and make test samples. Before leaving the store, however, record the label information for each fabric on an index card. You want to be able to find the exact fabric when you return to purchase the cloth. Facing four bolts of black cotton wondering which one gave that subtle salmon color can be most frustrating.

Begin your test by washing the sample fabrics in hot soapy water, rinsing, and drying. Divide each sample piece into six to eight strips. Take one strip and dip a section of it into a plastic or glass bowl containing a 50 percent bleach to 50 percent water solution. I start my testing with this ratio, but often find the solution isn't strong enough to discharge many of my samples. But seeing as the goal is to use the least amount of bleach to achieve the discharging, I start with this concentration and add bleach as necessary.

Keep careful notes on each index card as to how long the fabric took to discharge, the bleach concentration, and the colors that evolved as the bleach progressed. When the

10-6 First I dyed this fabric with many colors of fiber reactive dyes. After discharging selected areas, I went back in with more dye. I repeated the process several times, working quickly, carefully, and with progressively weaker bleach solutions.

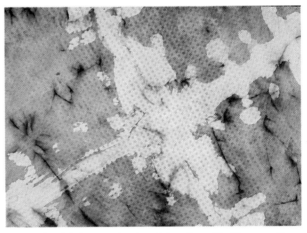

10-7 The fabric was dyed a pink color with fiber reactive dyes, folded into a bundle, and then dipped into the bleach only at its edges. The amount of bleach the fabric was allowed to absorb determined how much of the pink was removed.

strip reaches a color you like, immediately place it in the neutralizer to stop the action.

If the fabric color didn't change at all on some of your strips, mix up a stronger solution, take a new strip of that color, and try again. Continue adding small increments of bleach to the solution until you get the results you want. If the fabric simply doesn't change color at all, eliminate it from your choices. After neutralizing, washing, and drying the samples, attach them to your index cards for future reference.

Once you've identified the fabrics that will discharge, you can return to the fabric store and purchase the amount for your project.

Discharging Procedure

1. Prepare the washed fabric for discharging. Almost any technique in this book can be used to create a discharge pattern if you substitute bleach for the coloring agent. Try braiding, wax resists, stamping, painting, leaf printing, and compression techniques. I try to avoid spraying bleach, if possible, because I can't control where the bleach lands. I don't want it on me, surrounding objects, or my nearby plants. If your patterning process is slow, such as stamping with bleach, the areas discharged first will have a longer time to react producing lighter colors than those done more recently. So start with fairly short lengths of fabric.

2. Set up a process assembly line. A strong solution of bleach acts very quickly so each step must be carried out rapidly. Black fabric that discharges to the most wonderful coral must be plunged into the rinse water and neutralizer immediately to stop the color progress. Otherwise the bleach will continue to work until the coral color you liked so much has become a creamy tan.

   You can devise your own system, but mine is as follows: a rubber dishpan with the bleach solution, a bucket of water for the first rinse, a bucket of water for the second rinse, a bucket of neutralizer, and a final bucket of rinse water.

   Once everything is ready, and you've put on all your safety gear, start with the bleach solution. Add the liquid bleach to room temperature water in the proportions you determined from your previous tests. The fabric may either be wet first (best for some compression techniques) or dry. Either dip the fabric in the bleach, pour it over the fabric, paint or drip it on, or submerge for all over color lightening. Watch the fabric closely waiting for the color you liked on your test swatch. Sometimes the weather affects the speed of the bleaching action. Cold slows the bleach's progress. If you're working in full sun on a hot day, the bleach will react faster than a cloudy, cold day.

   When your fabric changes to the color you've been waiting for, immediately plunge it into the first bucket of rinse water. Agitate well and squeeze out the excess water. Now place the fabric quickly into a second bucket of clean water and rinse again. Then submerge the cloth in the third bucket containing the neutralizer. Agitate for about five minutes. The fabric can remain in the neutralizer without damage (no more than 35 minutes) giving you time to discharge the next piece of cloth. I usually try to work within color groupings as I find that some of the discharging color bleeds into the neutralizing solution and could re-deposit. Remove the fabric from the neutralizer, and place in the last bucket of rinse water to remove the neutralizer. Then machine wash and dry the fabric. To prevent any damage to the brushes or implements I used during the bleaching process, I also give them a dip into the neutralizer, followed by a thorough water rinse to be sure all chemicals have been removed.

   The chlorine discharge process is now completed. At this point, you can over-dye the fabric, paint new colors into the discharged areas, use the fabric as a base for additional surface design techniques, or store your fabric for future use.

DEVORÉ OR BURN-OUT TECHNIQUE

In discharged patterns, our goal was to control the destruction of color without harming the fiber. In the devoré technique, however, our aim is to destroy and remove the fiber. *Devoré* is a French word for devour or destroy, but I think of it as fire in a bottle. One puts the paste on the fabric, applies heat, and the fiber is quickly reduced to ash-like fragments.

But this is not true for all fabrics. The devoré paste is particular and removes only cellulose fibers such as cotton, viscose rayon, ramie, and linen. Synthetic fibers (polyester, nylon, and metallic) and protein fibers (silk and wool) are safe from its burning fire. Immediately we can see how this unique characteristic has potential for making patterns on fabric. The designer can choose a cellulose fabric if a total burn-out is wanted, or a mixed content fabric if only half of the fiber is to be removed (the cellulose threads) and the other half left intact (the synthetic or protein).

The ingredient that removes the cellulose fibers is sodium bisulfate, or as it is often called in Europe, sodium hydrogen sulfate. This highly acidic ingredient (pH-1) is added to a thickener to create a paste. You can purchase the paste ready-to-use as Fiber-Etch® fabric remover (Silkpaint Corporation). I prefer to use this premixed paste as it comes in a convenient squeeze bottle with a good drawing tip; and I don't have to store the chemicals. However, if you plan to use the paste in large quantity, you may want to mix your own. The recipe, glycerin, and industrial gum thickener needed to make the paste are available from Silkpaint Corporation. The sodium bisulfate can be purchased from a

10-8 In this assortment of samples, Fiber-Etch™ was used in two ways. (1) Remove fibers completely (cut work) on cellulose fabrics or (2) Remove only the cotton from a synthetic/cotton blend to create transparent areas (the gray colors in the photo). The stitch designed fabrics were created by Iris Lee and the abstract fabrics (lower half) by the author using compression techniques on azeta cloth from Silkpaint Corp.

pool supply store as a pH decreaser for spas and hot tubs. The one I use is "Bio Guard, SPA Guard." Others are available, but check the label to be sure they contain sodium bisulfate. The devoré paste has numerable uses:

1. To remove areas enclosed by a resist (fabric paint, iron-on appliqués, wax, or machine embroidery) for cutwork patterns without any frayed edges.

   When using fabric paint, the paint must penetrate to the backside of the fabric. Allow the paint to dry completely and then apply the paste next to the paint lines. Dry the devoré paste promptly with a hair dryer. As ironing to activate the devoré paste might flatten the paint line, a heat gun moving over the backside of the fabric can be substituted (beware of scorching). Be sure to check the manufacturer's instructions to confirm that your paint can be subjected to high heat safely though.

   If stitching is used as a barrier, your thread should be 100 percent polyester, nylon, silk, or metallic so it won't be devoured by the paste. Metallic thread should have a polyester, not a rayon core. Most of the flat "tinsel" threads are polyester and metallic.

   According to the Silkpaint experts, a design should be satin stitched onto the fabric using a stitch length of approximately .50 mm. Then stitch a width of at least $^1/_{16}$" so the paste will stay within the enclosed area. They also warn that some blue, or blue-toned acrylic thread dyes change color when touched by the devoré paste. So always test your thread first. When ironing to activate paste, metallic and acrylic threads may need a lower temperature for a longer time because of their content.

   Quilted pieces with satin stitched design areas can also be burned-out if cotton quilt batting and cotton fabrics are used. As the quilted sandwich will be thick, you need to apply the paste to both the front and back of the satin stitched design areas. The paste will eat through one layer at a time and not destroy the stitched areas if the proper thread is used.

2. To burn-out shaped holes in cellulose fabric by drawing onto the fabric with the paste without any resist barriers. The end result will be intentionally frayed, ragged shapes creating a "distressed" look.

3. To create transparent and opaque areas on a piece of mixed fiber cloth. This works especially well on lightweight, white fabric for a subtle contrast of whites, and on rayon/cotton velvets for a textural contrast.

4. To change the structural strength of the cloth. Removing all, or some of the woven fibers in areas causes those sections to collapse, or become less firm.

5. To make clean edged reverse appliqué without using a scissors. If two different fabrics are satin stitched together (for example, cotton on top and polyester on the bottom) and the devoré paste is applied to the top cotton layer, it will disappear and reveal the polyester fabric underneath.

Fabric

As in discharging, if you are using store bought fabrics, purchase a small amount and test it at home first. How a cloth is woven (which fiber is the weft and which is the warp) can be very important to the final effect, especially in blends. Avoid selecting fabrics with surface finishes or patterns that have been heavily printed with pigments. With fiber blends, I find that the cellulose content needs to be at least 50 percent to get clean burn-out patterns.

   Your best chance of success is to use those fabrics recommended for devoré by the fabric suppliers listed in this book. Silkpaint Corporation sells a 55" wide, white, 50 percent poly/cotton blend called azeta that I especially like. This batiste-weight fabric from England becomes very translucent in the burned-out areas. Other good combinations

10-9 On this vest, Iris Lee stitched through two layers of cellulose fabric. Then she used Fiber-Etch in the stitch enclosed areas to burn-out both layers. In the background fabric, the author drew with Fiber-Etch on 100% cotton fabric. Without any resist (stitching, paint) to block the solution, she got the frayed X pattern she wanted.

are 50/50 silk/linen, silk/cotton, wool/rayon, cotton/polyester, and silk/rayon velvet.

Method

When working with the devoré paste, mixing your own, or heat activating the paste, be sure to wear protective gear (gloves, respirator, eye goggles). The sodium bisulfate can be irritating to the eyes, skin, nose, and throat.

1. Secure your fabric to newspapers with tape or pins, or stretch it in an embroidery hoop. Shake the plastic squeeze bottle, or stir the devoré paste well. Apply the paste in a thin layer (not raised) from the tapered spout or paint it onto the right side of the fabric. Allow to air dry. A hair dryer can be used to dry small or detailed areas, but large areas take so long that I prefer to let the fabric dry overnight. If you unintentionally spot the fabric, apply baking soda to the still damp area or wash with soap and water before it dries.

Besides applying the paste by hand, an Air Pen™ from Silkpaint can be used. It works like a fat pen connected to an electric air pump and disperses a continuous flow of the devoré paste. Other mediums such as fabric paint, resists, and thickened dyes can also be run through the pen for long and flowing, drawn lines.

2. Protect your ironing surface with paper. Lay your fabric on top, face down and cover with a piece of thin fabric or tissue paper to protect your iron. Although the paste won't stick to the iron, it can discolor the metal. The falling out fibers can also collect in the steam holes. Begin to iron the fabric on the reverse side. Use a wool setting or a temperature appropriate to your fabric and iron. Do not use steam. I always do this procedure outside to ensure adequate ventilation.

3. When the pasted areas have turned a cafe-au-lait color (light brown), the chemical action is complete. Do not overheat or over iron the fabric. The pasted areas will feel brittle to the touch when sufficient heat has been applied.

4. Place the fabric under a gently running faucet to rinse away the fiber fragments from the pasted areas. You may need to lightly rub with your fingers some areas to remove all the burned-out fibers and residual paste.

If you are using a blend fabric, but find that both the cellulose and other fibers have been removed, try the process again. This time, use less devoré paste and less heat. The devoré technique is an industrial method done under very controlled conditions. Sometimes, we need to experiment several times with the same fabric to discover the exact amount of paste, the correct temperature setting time with our equipment, and the right color tone of the burned-out areas to achieve the same success as a commercial producer.

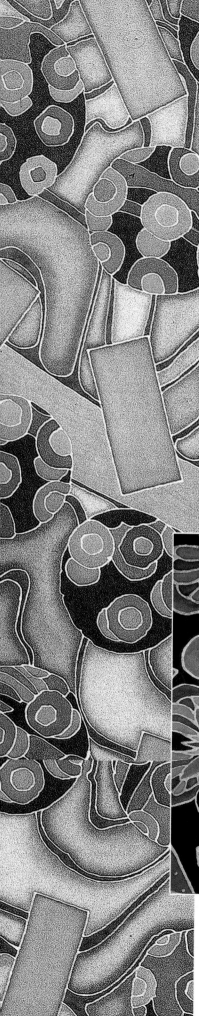

Chapter 11

WAX PATTERNS

Batik is the first word that comes to most minds when a hot wax technique is mentioned. Inspired by the exquisite beauty of Indonesian fabrics, many of us embarked on insanely ambitious batik projects. After days of dyeing and waxing, we ended up with permanently colored bathtubs, clogged drains from solidified wax, and a closet full of board-like fabrics that never would release all their wax.

Yet I have wonderful memories. I think of the process as a "grandmother technique" as it taught me so much about dyeing, the labor required, and respect for the craft. Whenever I come across a scrap from my batiked curtains, or a photo of my singed Berkeley kitchen burned by exploding wax, I still smile. I think everyone should try batik, at least once for the stories, and to develop a real appreciation for the simpler technique of dye painting with wax resist lines.

DYE PAINTING WITH WAX RESIST

In batik you save color areas by covering them in hot wax before submerging the fabric in a dye bath. Although the saved colors remain bright, the back-

11-1 *Metamorphosis Coat* (facing page and detail above), by Carolyn Dahl and Lisa Sharp. Hand-painted cotton and rayon velvet, fiber reactive dyes with wax resist, embellished with appliqué, quilting, sequins, and jewels.

116

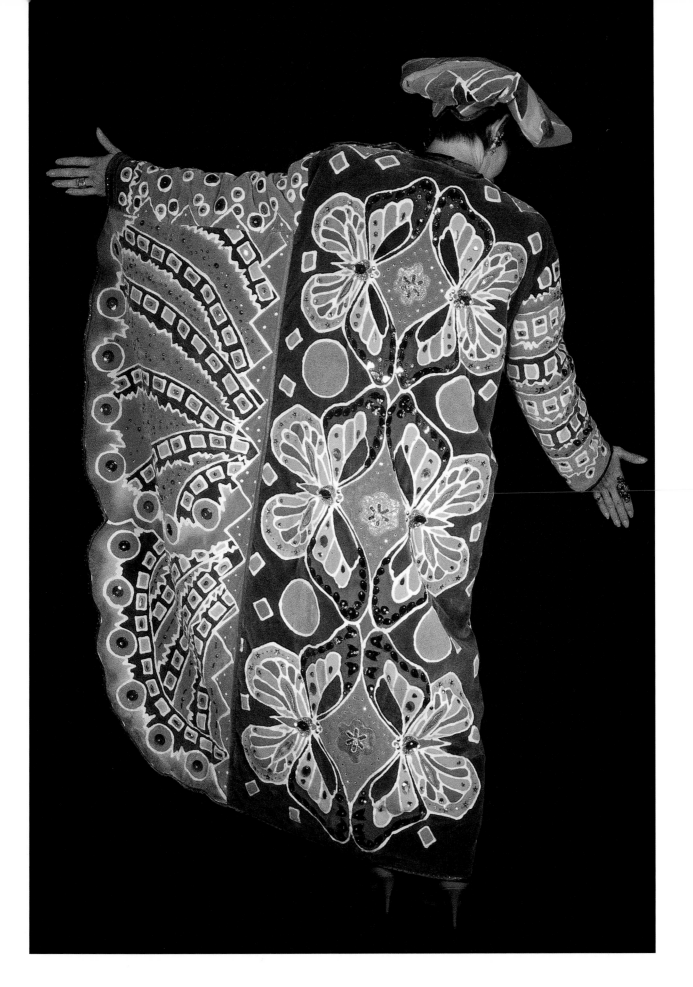

ground can turn muddy after about four to five dye baths. It's extremely difficult to achieve color variety when one color is constantly dyed on top of another. But in dye painting, the area you want to dye is outlined, not covered with wax, and the color painted into or around the shape, much like a stained glass window. As the fabric is never immersed, you can add as many colors as you desire, in any sequence, and still have a brilliantly colored final product. You must like the look of a drawing, however, as the lines surrounding each shape will always be an integral part of the final design.

Process Overview

To create a design, hot wax is applied to the fabric with a tjanting tool. Similar to a thick pencil, it has a metal cup at one end to hold the hot wax, a spout through which the wax flows, and a wooden or bamboo handle (Fig. 11-1 below). Think of it as a pen for writing, except the ink is hot wax. Tjanting tools may be manual or electric, with different size spout openings (small, medium, large, and extra large) depending on the width of the line to be drawn. Some have multiple spouts, up to seven, for drawing those perfect parallel lines we see in Indonesian batiks.

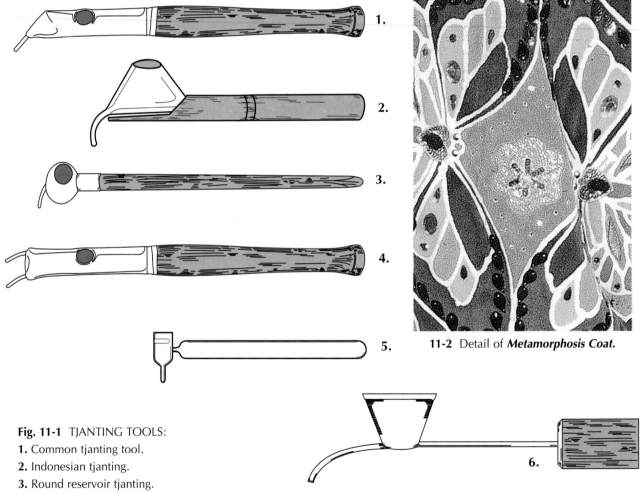

1.

2.

3.

4.

5.

6.

11-2 Detail of ***Metamorphosis Coat.***

Fig. 11-1 TJANTING TOOLS:
1. Common tjanting tool.
2. Indonesian tjanting.
3. Round reservoir tjanting.
4. Double-spouted tjanting.
5. Pyssanka tool for Ukrainian batik Easter eggs. Good for signatures and very fine details.
6. Large tjanting for covering areas with wax or making very wide lines.

Wherever the wax line is drawn, the color of the fabric is preserved underneath as the dye cannot penetrate the wax barrier, nor spread beyond the outline. Liquid fiber reactive dyes are brushed into the unwaxed areas while the fabric is horizontal, stretched over a frame, or on harite (page 125). Once dry, the fabric is heat-set to make the dyes permanent, and the wax is removed. If your original fabric was white, all your painted shapes will be outlined in white. If the fabric was multicolored, the lines will be multicolored after wax removal. Excess dye is then washed out and the fabric is ready to use.

Planning Your Design

You can draw your design freehand on the fabric, but I prefer to develop it first on paper and then trace it with wax onto the fabric. Cut a sheet of paper the size you want your finished work to be. Inexpensive drawing paper or the dull side of butcher paper may be used.

Do not use glossy paper as the wax will bead up on it and smear the design during waxing. The size of your design should match the size of the frame. Draw your design on the paper in pencil. Don't make your lines too close together, or the shapes too detailed as the wax line will spread somewhat. One line should always finish by connecting to another. If the shape is not totally enclosed by a wax outline, the dye will not be contained within the shape. Once you have a finished drawing, go over the lines with a black permanent marker (like a laundry pen) so you can see them easily. Allow the drawing to dry completely.

Transferring the Drawing to Cloth

Beginners should start with a smoothly woven cotton or viscose rayon fabric. Silks or textured fabrics such as velvet require more experience to achieve good results. For lightweight fabrics, you can transfer the drawing while applying the hot wax resist with the

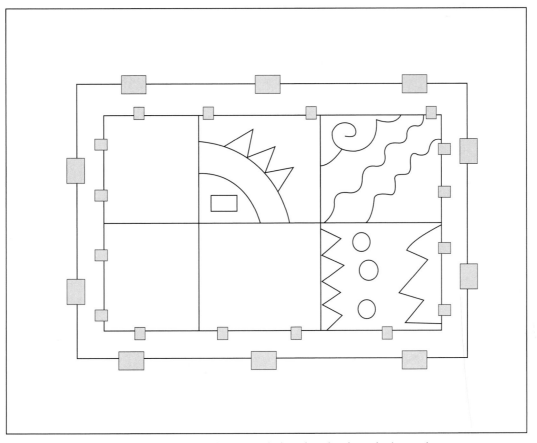

Fig. 11-2 Transferring design to cloth. Fabric has been laid over the paper drawing and the waxing process begun.

119

Fig. 11-3 Attaching the waxed fabric on the frame. The waxed fabric has been stretched over the frame, secured with push pins, and elevated in preparation for painting.

11-3 The designs have been transferred to velvet fabric with a tjanting tool and hot wax. Because of the fabric's nap, it took 3-4 days to wax all the sections using a wide resist line to ensure complete saturation. Once the fabric was stretched with harite, the painting process could begin.

tjanting tool. In this method, place the drawing on a smooth surface. Protect the surface with an old bed sheet or wax paper as the hot wax may penetrate the drawing. Lay the fabric over the drawing; the black lines should be visible through the fabric. Secure the drawing and fabric with masking tape to prevent shifting. Then trace the drawing's lines with the tjanting tool full of hot wax (see Fig. 11-2, page 119).

An alternative method is to wax the fabric while it is stretched on the frame instead of laying flat on a surface (see Fig. 11-3, above). The drawing is pinned to the backside of the fabric and removed after waxing. Some artists prefer this method because the fabric is stretched before the waxing, which reduces the possibility of breaking a waxed line while stretching. Try both methods and decide which works best for you and your design. For instance, if I am doing a very precise, detailed image, I find I have more control over the tjanting tool if I can rest my arm on a hard surface, instead of working over a frame edge on a suspended fabric.

If the fabric is so dense that you are unable to see your paper design, you can draw directly on the fabric with a soft charcoal stick or an Ebony pencil. Tracing over the drawing with Sulky® transfer pens and ironing the design onto the fabric also works. The Sulky pen lines, however, will become permanent, so you need to incorporate them into your overall design. Disappearing transfer ink pens may also be used, but should be tested first as some inks become permanent on contact with hot wax or dye chemicals.

Selecting the Wax Resist

Although we tend to think of beeswax when we hear "wax," many synthetic waxes, or combination mixtures are available. In Indonesia, the wax resist recipes are kept secret. Although they may contain the basic beeswax and paraffin, many other ingredients such as gums and resins are added to suit the working methods of the individual artist.

Paraffin Wax

This petroleum-based wax found in grocery stores in the canning section, or available from dye suppliers comes in block form (1–10 lb. sizes) or as granules for use in electric tjanting tools. Best wax to use to achieve the traditional batik crackle effect as it has little flexibility. Melting point is 135° to 140° F.

Beeswax

Beeswax is the natural product of bees secreted in flakes from their wax glands. The Apis mellifera (honey-making bee) uses the wax to build combs in which to rear its young and store honey. Wax purchased from dye suppliers has been processed to remove all impurities and moisture left in the wax. Usually beeswax is blended with paraffin to reduce costs and because it is more flexible and does not crack or flake off as easily as pure paraffin. Working with beeswax is pleasant as it has a lingering fragrance reminiscent of its flower source and a beautiful creamy color. If you do your waxing outside near flowers, you may have a few bee visitors who seem to be drawn to their own beautiful product. Melting point is 130° F.

Microcrystalline Wax

This is a synthetic wax often substituted for beeswax. Also called sticky wax, it is a petroleum-based product that can be added to paraffin instead of the more expensive beeswax. Microcrystalline wax comes in one pound blocks and has a melting point of 160 to 170° F.

Batik Wax

Usually a blend of 25 percent microcrystalline wax with 75 percent paraffin, it is sold premixed in granulated form. Easy to melt, it's perfect for electric tjantings. Melting point is 150° F.

If you have any allergies to wax fumes or respiratory sensitivities, water soluble resists or gutta serti (see Silk Painting, page 138) may be substituted for the wax, but only if a light to medium weight fabric is to be painted.

Applying the Wax Resist

I use a mixture of half paraffin and half beeswax. If you like, you can melt your wax in a double boiler, but an electric frying pan with a thermostatic control works better as it maintains an even temperature. I set the dial to 160 to 225° F. The temperature depends on the fabric. A thicker one needs a little higher temperature to penetrate the dense fibers; whereas, thin fabric requires a lower temperature to control wax spreading. Always have adequate ventilation when heating the wax. Place the pan near a kitchen stove's exhaust fan (protect your stove from drips), or better yet, work in an open garage or outside as I do.

Never leave the wax unattended! If the phone rings, or you are finished for the day, shut off the pan and pull out the plug. You don't want any photos of burned kitchens in your album. Most of us tend to think of wax as a harmless substance found in crayons, food, cosmetics, and candles. But like fat in a

11-4 *Space Stream #2* by Carolyn Dahl. Dye painting with wax resist on silk habutai, 45" x 80".

frying pan, it is combustible and can cause a fire. If it begins to smoke, turn down the temperature immediately. Keep a box of baking soda and the pan's lid nearby to smother flames should they ever occur. Never place a pot of wax directly on an open flame. My fire occurred because the gas flame under the pan in which I had the wax did not go out totally when I shut off the burner and left the room. The pan probably heated at least half an hour before it ignited and taught me a hard lesson.

Wax can also burn your skin. If the tjanting slips into the hot wax, use an implement to retrieve it. Wax clings to the skin so the burning time is increased, making even a small splatter quite painful. So keep your fingers away from the wax and children and pets out of the room.

Used properly and watched closely, wax is not dangerous and shouldn't scare you. The key is knowing the risk and then following procedures to eliminate it. Wax has been used for centuries. I am one of the rare few who have ever seen it throw fireballs.

Using the Tjanting Tool

Batik may very well owe its name to the mark of the tjanting tool.[1] The characteristic use of the tjanting tool in the designing of Indonesian fabrics is to outline a pattern in tiny drops of wax. *Tik* refers to drop, point, or little bit, thus a fabric called batik has in its name the process by which it was made. Batik can also mean wax writing[2], and as the tjanting is often called a wax pen, the tool's mark and the cloth's name do seem linked in origin.

The word *tjanting* is a visually interesting word. Unfortunately, the Indonesian government has modernized its language and officially changed tjanting to canting tool. I, however, plan to remain old fashioned and continue using the more exotic spelling. I hope you will too. When a name seems to fit the personality and cultural history of the tool, I hate to let it disappear from the dyer's vocabulary.

Even though the name may be old fashioned, the tool need not be. Today one can choose to use the traditional manual tjanting tool, or the modern electric version. If you don't mind always being connected to a cord, the electric tjanting has several advantages. The wax flakes or granules are fed directly into the heated reservoir, so you do not need to tend a wax pot and fumes are minimal. The wax in the reservoir is kept at a constant temperature because of a built-in thermostat so the wax flow is steadier than in a hand-dipped tjanting. Although the time may vary, most manufacturers claim that one filling will last from 5 to 10 minutes, which means that longer lines can be drawn with fewer breaks. The electric tjanting is compact, and as no wax pot is needed, less studio storage space is required.

With a manual tjanting, the waxer must control more variables. Working with the tool can be a beautiful process, but it does require some practice and concentration because it is a more primitive tool. The control is in the hand, not technology.

Dip the manual tjanting's metal reservoir into the hot wax; hold it submerged until all the hardened wax from your last work session has melted and the reservoir is clear. When the hot wax flows freely through the spout, fill the tjanting about $3/4$ full. As you lift it out of the wax, have a folded paper towel (or plastic spoon, jar lid) in your other hand to place under the spout to catch drips. Keep the wax pan near your fabric to lessen the chance of the wax cooling in the reservoir.

Move the tjanting to your starting point on the fabric and remove the towel to release the flow of wax. Work quickly and skim over the surface making sure that all lines connect. Do not press the tip down hard against the fabric or the wax will stop flowing. Your goal is to achieve a long, continuous line of wax. As you wax each shape, try to progress from the left to the right of the fabric to assure that any wrinkles produced will be released at the fabric's edge. When the tjanting needs to be refilled, replace the towel under the spout as you move over the fabric back to the wax pan.

Look closely at the waxed lines on your fabric. If the wax has penetrated the fibers, it will look translucent and smooth, almost transparent. If it has a milky, rough, opaque look, the wax needs to be hotter to penetrate completely. Also remember to watch for breaks in the lines where dye might escape into unwanted areas. If working on stretched fabric, you can hold the frame up to the light, which makes seeing the line breaks easier. To correct a break, wax over the exact spot on the backside of the fabric.

Don't be discouraged if at first your lines are wobbly and the tjanting tool feels awkward. With time you will understand its ways. Sometimes two or three tjantings must be tried to find the one that seems to match your hand.

Even though you are tracing a design, be aware of the expressive quality of the wax and tool. The results will contain your gestures and reflect your mood like handwriting. Working with hot wax is not a process you do when agitated or distracted. In fact, Indonesian women often meditate to reach the proper state in which to begin work[3] because they know how responsive the tjanting is to one's temperament. Good work is only possible "on a good day with tools that were blessed."[4] In a book by Nancy Belfer, craftsman Aisjah Soedarsono sums up the connection between one's spirit and the work with these words: "We batik both sides. It's part of the old Javanese philosophy that holds that a person should be the same inside and out. In other words, be honest to himself. During the time you work on batik, you shouldn't talk. Your feelings should be quiet and clear."[5]

STRETCHING THE FABRIC ON THE FRAME

If you waxed on a flat surface, remove the tape and gently separate the drawing from the waxed fabric. Work slowly to avoid cracking the lines. Lay the fabric over canvas stretcher bars (available in art supply stores) or an adjustable frame. Attach the fabric with push-pins while stretching it gently for even tension. Do not pull so hard that the wax cracks or the fabric is pulled off grain. When attached all around, there should be no low spots and the fabric should spring back to the touch. It will sag when wet, so if you are working with a small frame on a flat surface, you may need to elevate your frame by placing some object under each side (cat food tins, shoe boxes, bricks) (See Fig. 11-3, page 120).

If the piece is very large, a make-shift frame can be made by laying two boards (spaced to the width of your fabric) across two saw horses or supports. Secure the boards with C-clamps, and you have a large, easy-to-make and store frame.

Another stretching option is to sling the fabric hammock style. The Japanese use harite, which are wooden clamps that run the full width of each end of the fabric. Think of them as jaws (two boards hinged together) that bite down on the fabric with metal teeth (small nails that fit into holes) to hold the fabric while it is being stretched lengthwise, or with the warp (Fig. 11-4, facing page). As harite are easy to make yourself, I have many sets that match the various widths of the fabrics I use the most. However, if you plan to purchase only one set, get the longest size (60") which will accommodate all fabric widths (John Marshall supplies).

Even after the fabric is stretched lengthwise on the harite, it will still have some ripples running from selvage to selvage. Thus shinshi, which are bamboo sticks with sharp needle-like points in each end, are inserted in the fabric selvages across the width (woof) at intervals. Because the shinshi length is slightly greater than the fabric length (approximately 2 to 2 1/2" longer), the flexible bamboo bends, causing enough tension in the fabric to straighten out the ripples.

Before I discovered a source for the Japanese harite and shinshi, I devised my own method (see Figure 11-5, page 126). I wrapped 1" dowels in a heavy, fat fabric to create a padded surface. Then I pinned the fabric to be painted onto this padded dowel with straight or safety pins (double over the fabric edge to prevent rips), put ring hooks on each end of the dowels to run a strong cord through, and connected the cords to hooks (or a hammock stand) to stretch the fabric length. Instead of bamboo shinshi, which work the best because of their flexibility, I have substituted the thinnest wooden dowels available, pounded a T-pin into each end, cut off the T, and had my own version of shinshi.

As I am often leaning against the fabric edge to paint, I also put a small cork over the metal points to protect my stomach.

Painting the Fabric

This is the exciting part. Load either an inexpensive watercolor brush or a foam rubber applicator with dye. Touch the brush to the center of a white area and watch the dye spread until it bumps into a wax barrier. The dye will be darkest where it is first applied and become lighter as it spreads through the fabric. Add as many colors as you like, but don't be influenced in your color mixings by the light golden color of the waxed lines. Remember, once the wax is removed, these lines will return to white.

When the dyes are dry, additional wax lines or shapes can be added to divide painted

Directions for Making Homemade Harite

1. Purchase four pieces of unfinished wood, either ³⁄₄" x ¹⁄₂" or 2" x ¹⁄₂". Cut each piece 8" to 10" longer than your fabric width. You will need two boards per set.

2. Mark the top board of each set with these measurements:

For cord holes: 1" to 1¹⁄₂" in from each end
For nail holes: ¹⁄₂" to 1" intervals across length

3. Lay each marked board on top of an unmarked board and clamp ends together with C clamps. Hammer thin, sharp nails into the top board following your nail hole marks. The nails should be long enough to go completely through the top board and into the bottom board about ¹⁄₄" to ³⁄₈". Drill the cord holes completely through both boards.

4. Remove the clamps and pry the two boards apart. The top board will have nails protruding from it and the bottom board will have matching holes. If you have difficulty with this system, you can do the boards separately. Pound the nails through the top board, press it to the bottom board to make nail indentations, and then drill out the nail holes and cord holes separately.

5. Add 2 or 3 hinges to one side of the set to connect the two boards and make the "jaw." Run a strong cord or rope through the cord holes. The traditional method is to thread one end of the cord through the top of one side and the bottom of the other. This method helps keep the clamps from popping open. I, however, like to look at my work in a vertical position. So I avoid the knots, and run the cord under the bottom board so I can slide the harite in any direction I choose. To keep the harite closed, I use masking tape or loop the cord around each end.

6. Center the fabric over the metal teeth. Attach one end of the fabric to a metal point, stretch it slightly over the other points, and attach to the last point it reaches. Close the harite and the teeth will penetrate the fabric.

7. Connect your cord to another cord that will attach to a hook, post, or hammock stand for slinging the fabric. If the second cord has a slip knot you can adjust your fabric's tautness as you work.

8. Insert the shinshi along the width of the fabric and you're ready to paint.

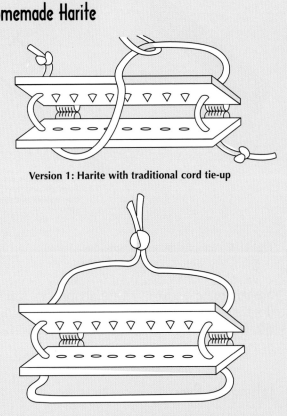

Version 1: Harite with traditional cord tie-up

Version 2: Author's cord tie-up so harite can be moved to a vertical position for viewing fabric.

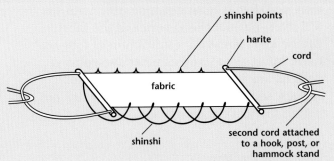

Fabric stretched between poles with harite and shinshi

Fig. 11-4 Japanese harite for stretching fabric.

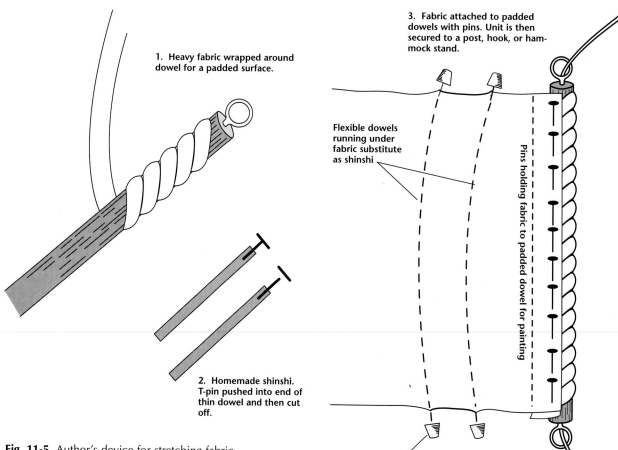

1. Heavy fabric wrapped around dowel for a padded surface.

2. Homemade shinshi. T-pin pushed into end of thin dowel and then cut off.

3. Fabric attached to padded dowels with pins. Unit is then secured to a post, hook, or hammock stand.

Flexible dowels running under fabric substitute as shinshi

Pins holding fabric to padded dowel for painting

Small corks placed over cut off T-pin points

Fig. 11-5 Author's device for stretching fabric.

areas, create texture within shapes, or clarify details. These new lines will be colored when the wax is removed as the fabric they were drawn on was already painted.

Setting the Dyes

The best setting methods for waxed fabric are ironing and steam setting because while you are setting the fabric, most of the wax is also removed. Batch setting can be used with the MX dyes, but not the H series, if the fabric can be kept moist for a minimum of four or more hours. However, as most dye-painted designs are rather complex, with smaller shapes, sections of the fabric usually dry out before the work is completed.

Removing the Wax

The amount of wax to remove from the fabric will be less in the dye painting process than in batik as only the outlines contain wax.

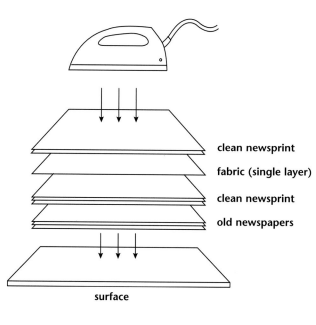

clean newsprint

fabric (single layer)

clean newsprint

old newspapers

surface

Fig. 11-6 Removing wax by ironing

However, even a small amount of wax needs to be removed or the fabric will feel stiff.

As already mentioned, ironing the fabric will not only heat set it but also remove most of the wax (see Fig. 6). Protect your ironing board or other surface with old newspapers. Be sure the newspapers are old or the ink may transfer when heated. Cover the newspaper with layers of clean newsprint (or whatever is abundant such as packing paper, tissue paper, or paper towels). Lay your fabric on top of the paper and cover with several layers of clean newsprint, or substitute. Now iron slowly at the hottest temperature your fabric can tolerate. Remember you are heat setting the dyes at the same time so iron according to the directions on page 18. When the papers are saturated with melted wax, change the layers and repeat the process until the paper no longer picks up melted wax. Move to a new area and repeat the process. The melting wax will fume somewhat so have good ventilation in the room and wear a respirator.

If you steam set your fabric, most of the wax will be absorbed by the paper surrounding it. In both setting methods, however, some wax will still remain in the fabric, visible as dark rings around the shapes and a stiffness to the fibers.

Although it is possible to remove the residue with purchased solvents, I recommend taking it to a dry cleaner for your safety and ease. Some dry cleaners are reluctant to accept hand-painted fabric as they fear the wax and bleeding dye will ruin their solvents, which are reused. If so, you might ask if they would run your fabric through just before they clean their solutions. If you heat set your fabric first, rinse it thoroughly so that no dye bleeds out, and remove as much of the wax as humanly possible before bringing it in, your fabric shouldn't cause any problems and the dry cleaner will soon trust you.

If however, they still refuse, and you are the type who likes to have the last word, you might remind them that they owe their business to the very same wax you want removed from your fabric. Back in 1825, Jean Batiste Jolly, a Frenchman, noticed that spilled wax from a paraffin lamp removed some stains on a tablecloth.[6] With that observation, he got the idea to clean clothing using wax as the solvent. Benzene soon replaced paraffin, and later more modern day solvents were developed, but wax started the whole industry. I can't guarantee that this tidbit of cleaning history will change their minds, but it does seem to throw them off balance, giving you time to gather up your precious fabric and make a graceful exit.

If you do not want to use a dry cleaner, and have a sturdy fabric (not silk), you can try the Indonesian method of wax removal by boiling the fabric and skimming off the melting

11-5 *Carolyn's Cows Break Loose at the Dance* by Carolyn Dahl. Dye painting with wax resist on silk habutai, 45" x 72".

127

wax as it rises to the water's surface. I find the process very slow. But if you do use it, do not pour the hot water containing liquid wax down the drain as the wax could collect in your pipes. Instead, allow the water to cool and the wax will solidify into an easily removed sheet. The wax is not reusable as the boiling destroys some of its adhesive properties.

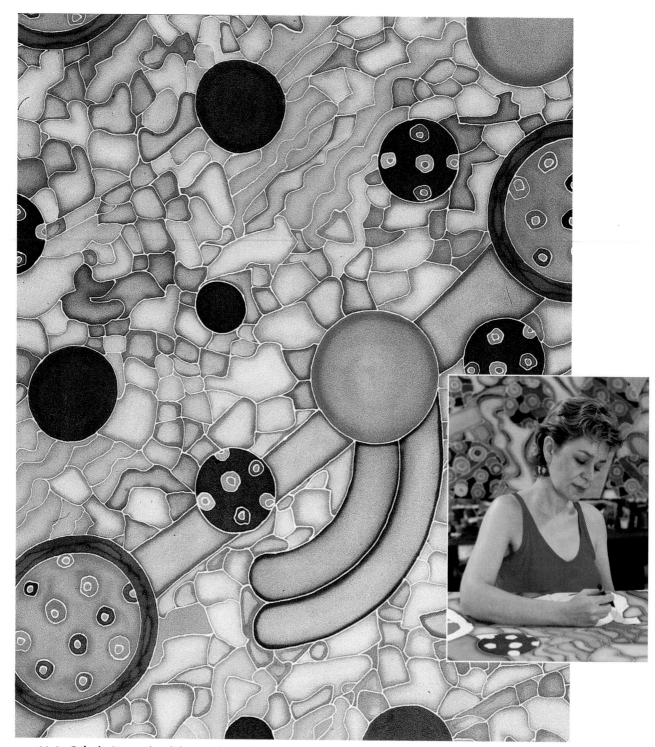

11-6 *Galaxie Storm* (detail) by Carolyn Dahl. Dye painting with wax resist on silk habutai, 45" x 80".
11-7 Above right, Carolyn Dahl painting *Galaxie Storm*, with *Space Stream #2* in the background (shown on page 122).

WAX STAMPING

Stamping is the drummer of techniques. Dyes flow quietly and gently into the fabric, but a wooden stamp hits the cloth with a sound. As the stamp repeats across the fabric, the sounds unite into a working rhythm.

In the past, rhythm and noise were a normal part of a textile worker's day. Drums and chants often helped to relieve the monotony of the tedious, repetitive work. I can only imagine the cacophony of sounds as workers banged wooden stamps against stones to knock off excess wax, pounded the backside of blocks to transfer paint to the fabric, and smacked the stamps against creaking tables while listening to drumming or chanting. No wonder so many old textiles feel like they are still throbbing with rhythm. The sound may be quieter now with only one hand stamping per studio. In fact, you may not even be aware of the rhythm when you start the process.

At first, the mind slowly directs the hand through each step: dip the stamp in the wax, tap off the excess against the pan, and press the stamp to the cloth. As you continue, however, a faster internal rhythm develops: dip, tap, press, dip, tap, press. You no longer think the process. Your mind falls silent as your body moves to its own trance-like beat.

If you have difficulty feeling the rhythm, you're probably being too timid. Whack your stamp on the wax pan harder to remind yourself of its noisy tradition. Or buy the wildest percussive tape you can find, chase everyone else out of the house, and move to the music's rhythm until yours awakens.[7]

Making Wax Stamps

Many found objects can be dipped into hot wax and printed directly. The only consideration is that the object can withstand the heat of the wax. For this reason, wood and metal are traditionally used for wax stamps. Wood will be the material we use, either as a precut or a hand-cut wood shape.

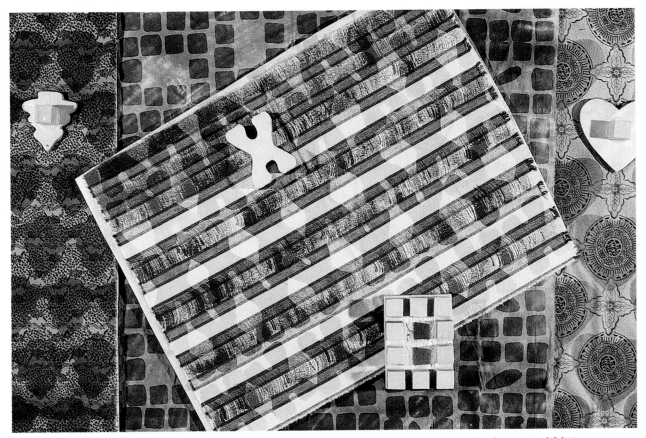

11-8. Felt-covered precut wood shapes were used to stamp wax designs onto previously painted or printed fabric.

Fig. 11-7 Craft and hobby stores sell a variety of unpainted, precut wood shapes that can be used as wax stamps.

Precut Wood Shapes

Unpainted, precut wood shapes can be found in most hobby or craft stores. Building a collection quickly is easy as they come in numerous shapes (hearts, lizards, stars), numbers, letters, and themes (Christmas, cowboy). To prepare them for use as a wax stamp, you simply trace the shape onto a piece of craft felt, cut out and glue the felt shape to the wood shape so it will absorb wax, add a handle to the opposite side, and your stamp is ready (Fig. 11-8, page 129).

Hand-cut Wood Shapes

More complex and personal stamps can be made if you design and cut your own wooden shapes. When planning a stamp design, remember that its power often lies in the pattern made when the image is repeated. So test designs you're considering by multiplying the image (trace or photocopy repeatedly and tape together to see the overall effect). If you want a continuous, interlocking stamped pattern like those used on commercial fabrics, refer to the textile design books listed in the chapter notes.[8]

1. Determine the size of your finished stamp. Stamps that are anywhere from a 2" to a 6" square are the easiest to use.

2. Draw your design on tracing paper. If your image has multiple parts, number each and allow a little space between each section to prevent wax fill in (Fig. 11-8).

11-9 Stamping on white fabric reserves a lot of white for a very crisp pattern. The wax may later be removed and additional colors painted into those reserved spaces. Original stamp design and fabric by Mary Ann Willey.

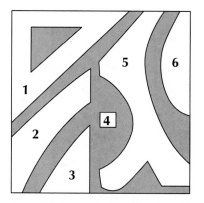

Fig. 11-8 Draw the design on tracing paper and number the pieces.

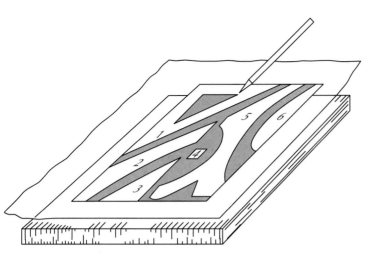

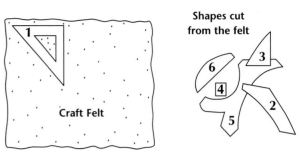

Fig. 11-10 Lay the cut out wood pieces on craft felt and trace around each shape. Cut out the shapes drawn on the felt.

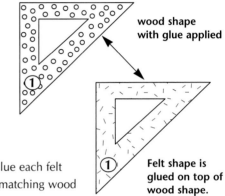

Fig. 11-9 Use carbon paper to transfer the stamp design to the wood. Cut out each shape with a saw.

Fig. 11-11 Glue each felt shape to the matching wood shape.

3. If you are satisfied with the design, trace it onto the wood from which you intend to cut the individual pieces (thin plywood or masonite are good choices). Carbon paper of any type can be used for the transfer (Fig. 11-9).

4. Cut the individual pieces out of the wood with an electric saw (band or scroll saw). Or if you want to avoid cutting the pieces yourself, you can take them to a woodworker. It helps to design many stamps at once, trace and number all the pieces on the wood yourself, and then request that the lines be followed as precisely as possible. Be sure to have some support blocks cut at the same time so you are ready to mount the pieces immediately. Support blocks should be $1/2$ to 1" thick to prevent warping and slightly larger than design.

5. Once all the pieces have been cut out, lay them on white craft felt and trace around the shapes (Fig. 11-10). In order for the wax to stay on the wood for stamping, the surface must be covered with an absorbent material such as felt. Cut out the shapes and glue them onto the matching wood shapes with a heat resistant glue (most wood glues will work). Allow to dry (Fig. 11-11).

6. Now trace the original design again, this time on the support block of wood. Then glue the felt-covered wood shapes onto the support block, matching the numbers of each piece. This will re-create your original design. Allow to dry (Fig. 11-12).

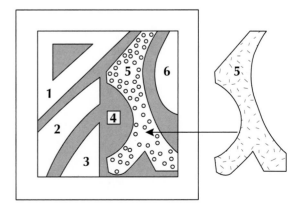

Fig. 11-12 Trace the original design onto the support block as a placement guide. Glue the individual felt-covered wood shapes onto the support block matching the shapes to the traced design. Allow to dry.

7. Turn the support block over and place a number on each of the four sides. These numbers will serve as guides if you rotate the design as you stamp. It is also helpful to trace the original design on the block. Be sure to reverse the drawing before tracing so it will be in the exact same position as the underside image. Now glue on a handle (small square of wood, thread spool) (Fig. 11-13). Your custom designed stamp is ready to meet the wax.

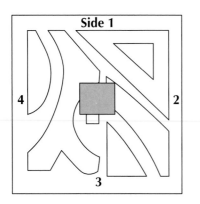

Side 1

4

2

3

Fig. 11-13 Turn the block over. Number all four sides and trace the original design in reverse on the block. Glue on a handle.

Wax Stamping Procedure

Before beginning to stamp with wax, return to the Dye Painting with Wax Resist section (page 121) for a review of hot wax safety, temperature control, and set up. The wax mixture (half paraffin and half beeswax), the heat setting methods, and wax removal will also be the same as those described in that section.

Whether you use a precut wood stamp or a hand cut design, the wax stamping procedure will be the same.

Cover the work surface with a thin layer of smooth newspaper. On top of this, place wax paper and then the washed and ironed fabric. Sometimes a short length of fabric needs to be taped at the edges so it won't lift with the stamp.

Submerge the felt portion of the stamp into the hot wax until it absorbs the liquid. Lift the stamp out and tap it against the side of the skillet to remove excess wax, or tilt it and let the overflow run back into the pan. Test the stamp on some scrap fabric. If the waxed image spreads too much, the wax is too hot. If the image appears milky and scratchy,

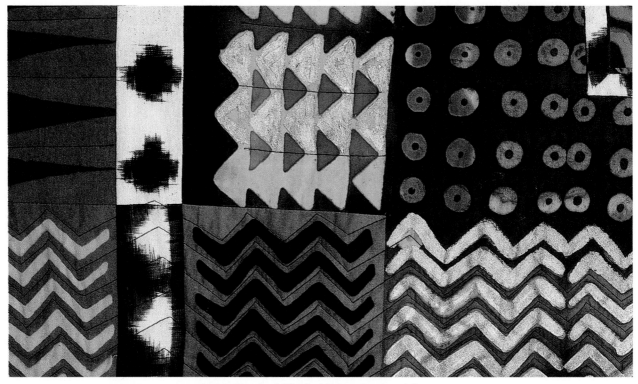

11-10 Detail of *Blocked Energy* by Ann Adams.

11-11 ***Blocked Energy***, a quilt by Ann Adams uses wax stamping in its design. Ann traces her shapes on balsa wood, which is soft enough to cut with a hand saw (coping or jewelers), and then mounts them on a plywood block.

11-12 When the painted fabric is separated from the wax paper on which it was laying, both are often very beautiful. The wax paper on the right picked up some newspaper print making the heart shapes even more interesting.

11-13 The fabrics after heat setting, wax removal, and washing.

11-14 Charlotte Peel painted the fabric first, wax stamped over the colors to reserve them, and then painted the background a rich brown. Stamp design and fabric by Charlotte Peel.

the wax temperature is too low or your stamp is too cold.

When your test images are well defined and the wax is penetrating properly, you are ready to begin. You may choose to stamp in a random pattern or a repeat. If you are doing a repeat pattern, guidelines can be sketched lightly on the fabric. But usually, just starting at a straight line such as the selvage or the top of the fabric, will be sufficient for a hand-produced fabric.

Try to develop a rhythm as you work: dip the stamp in the wax, tap off the excess, move quickly to the fabric, and come down straight

with the stamp. (If the stamp tilts, wax may run to the edge and drip onto your fabric). Lift the stamp off and repeat the procedure again.

As with the tjanting tool, avoid crossing over the fabric with a loaded stamp whenever possible. Although a lid or paper towel can be held under the stamp, the stamp's larger size makes the process very awkward and breaks the stamping rhythm. If you're having a problem with drips, you may wish to cover already waxed and unwaxed sections of the fabric with paper as a precaution.

How long to leave the stamp on the fabric

11-15 Sometimes the stained papers are so beautiful, they inspire a new artwork. *Fragments* (detail), by Carolyn Dahl.

and how much pressure to apply must be decided by you. Silk absorbs wax quickly and needs little transfer pressure. A thick cotton may require more pressure as it absorbs wax more slowly. If your stamp design has many large, unbroken surface areas, it will hold a lot of wax. Pressing too hard causes the wax to squish out the sides or fill in smaller design elements. After a few tests, however, you will know what the stamp needs from you by how it is printing.

After the wax is hard, the fabric is ready to paint. Leave the fabric adhered to the wax paper (they will have melted together) and start painting the unwaxed sections of your design.

When the dye is dry, and before heat setting, separate the fabric from the wax paper. This is one of my favorite moments.

Not only is the fabric beautiful as it glows with translucent waxed images, but also the paper that has absorbed the dye.

I never throw beauty away. Instead, I hang the dyed paper in a small round window on my second floor. During the day with the sun outside, it throws color into the room. At night my lights toss it outside. Neighbors tell me they often walk by at night just to see if a new "stained glass" window has appeared. Knowing they might be out there in the dark, I always leave a light burning. I like the idea of sharing a moment that happened during the process, instead of only the finished product. There may not be a drum sounding in my studio after wax stamping, but I like to think that the color is sending some kind of rhythm into the night.

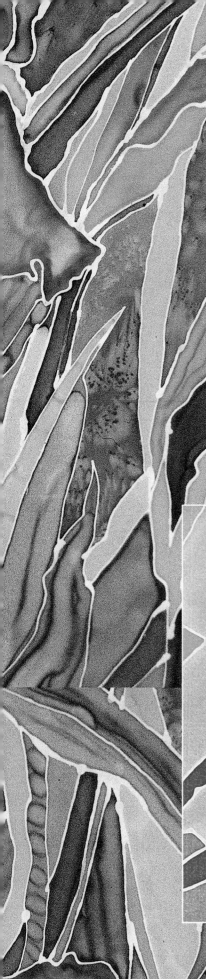

SILK PAINTING

Remember the haiku poem of the silkworm wrapped in her bed of silk dreaming herself a butterfly. In this technique, we answer the dream. We give her old bed, the cocoon now made into silk fabric, the colors she never would have had if she had emerged as a moth. The painted silk becomes the butterfly.

Silk painting is usually done with French dyes, so called because they originally referred to traditional French colors. Now the term is sort of generic indicating dyes that dilute with water and alcohol. Instead of the French dyes, we will substitute fiber reactive dyes. Some techniques listed in silk painting books will not work as well with fiber reactive dye, but the majority can be followed with good results.

The process steps are the same as those given in the Dye Painting with Wax Resist section except that the resist used will not be wax, but a solvent or water-based resist called gutta. Also, the fabric choice will be limited to silk and the techniques to those that are most effective on silk. As the fabric is a very important component in silk painting, let's cover it first.

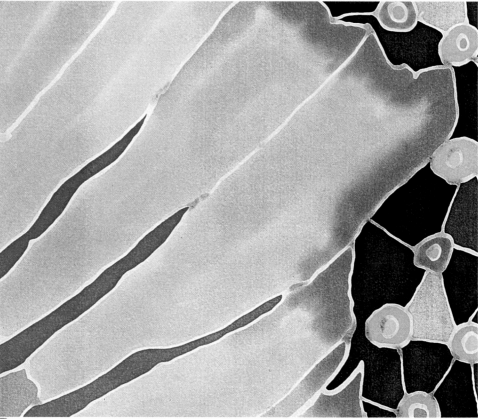

12-1 *Transformations* by Carolyn Dahl (detail above and facing page).
Fiber reactive dyes with gutta resist on silk. 45" x 72". Photo by Michael McCormick.

SILK FABRIC

The silk most used by fiber artists is habutai (also spelled habotae, habotai). Habutai, which means "soft as down"[1] in Japanese, is a lightweight, plain weave fabric with a smooth, lustrous surface that responds well to silk painting techniques. Although it is often called China silk, many sources do not agree that it is the exact same material.

According to the authors of *Sew Wonderful Silk*, China silk is made from "waste silk,"[2] such as the broken filaments from a pierced cocoon or the end of the cocoon. Because these short fibers have to be spun together to make yarn, the fabric has a different feel from reeled silk. China silk is a very lightweight fabric mainly used for lingerie, scarves, and linings.

Habutai silk, however, is reeled from the cocoon in long unbroken filaments, which are slightly twisted as it is spun into yarn. The result is a heavier, smoother, more opaque silk suitable for clothing and fiber works.

Whether you purchase the fabric as habutai or China silk, look for yardage with 8, 10, or 12 mommie weight. "Mommie" (mummie, momme, or mm) is an old Chinese term still used today to measure the weight of silk fabric and to remind us of silk's Oriental heritage. *The Art of Painting on Silk* states that "one mommie equals 4.3056 gm /5/32 oz. in weight to one square metre/yard of fabric... anything under 10 mommie is considered lightweight fabric"[3] over medium to heavyweight fabric.

Many silks other than habutai may also be used in silk painting as long as the gutta resist can penetrate the fabric. Broadcloth is a good beginner's cloth as it is easy to sew. Crepe de Chine is a beautiful material, but because it is woven from highly twisted yarns, the dye isn't absorbed as easily but must be worked somewhat into the fabric. Pongee has a slight tooth that holds the dye well, much like good watercolor paper.

Even transparent silks, such as chiffon and organza take color, but require more dye because of their open weave structure. Painting several layers at once will increase the dye's efficiency. If bold, simple shapes are painted, a patterned fabric such as a jacquard silk can add an interesting background to the images. And if you're looking for a rough textured silk that almost resembles cotton, silk noil is a good choice. The little black dots sprinkled across the fabric create a homespun look, but are in reality the remains of the chrysalis caught in the fibers.

One of my favorite fabrics is douppioni silk (or doupion, or the Japanese tamaito). The name is derived from an Italian word for double, because the fabric is made from the silk of two joined cocoons. Maybe it is true that crowding causes the worms to spin together, but I prefer Isabel Wingate's more poetic version: "Two silkworms . . . have an affinity for each other and want to stay together, so together they spin one cocoon."[4] Although the fabric has a characteristic slub to it, I still think it would be the perfect choice for a Valentine's day dress, or even a wedding dress.

GUTTA

Gutta means resist in French and comes in two types. The first is solvent soluble and is usually sold as gutta serti, with serti meaning enclosing. The second type is water soluble and called simply gutta, or a water-soluble resist. Both types of gutta are less fluid than wax, seldom drip, and spread very little. Thus your designs can be more complex and precise than those drawn with hot wax.

Solvent-Soluble Gutta

The solvent-soluble gutta resembles rubber cement and comes from trees of the Sapotacea family found in Borneo, Malaya, and Sumatra.[5] Occasionally it appears as *colle serti,* meaning gum or glue resist, but its most common name is gutta serti.

Sometimes the gutta serti you purchase is too thick and will not penetrate your fabric. It must then be thinned with a gutta dilutent or thinner sold by the manufacturer, or the recommended solvent (often white spirits). Add

The gutta serti can be applied with a squeeze bottle fitted with a plastic tip/metal nib (smaller number, smaller hole) or a paper cone. Gutta serti colorants may be purchased and added to the clear gutta for colored lines. Some brands can be colored yourself with oil-based paints or printing inks.

The best method to set the dyes after painting is steam setting, as the gutta serti can become sticky when heated. However, if you do set the dyes with an iron, protect your board and iron as if removing wax. I don't recommend dryer setting, as a solvent would be necessary to remove any gutta should it spot dryer parts, which would be dangerous. Batch setting may be used if the fabric has remained moist.

Solvent-based gutta can only be removed from the fabric by dry cleaning. Do not, however, dry clean the colored and metallic guttas. The solvents would dissolve or change the color (black turns gray). As these special guttas are left in the fabric permanently, all the lines should be drawn as fine as possible.

Applying Gutta Serti with a Plastic Bottle

Fill the plastic squeeze bottle with gutta serti completely to the top to eliminate air bubbles. Some bottles come with a plastic tip, others with the metal nib already attached, and some you will need to attach the nib to the plastic cap (wrap a piece of tape around the connection point to prevent separation). Gently squeeze the bottle just enough to bring the gutta up into the spout to eliminate trapped air. Test the consistency on a scrap fabric piece.

If the gutta serti is flowing well, move to your fabric and place the nib where you wish to begin and squeeze gently and steadily. Try for a smooth continuous line with the least amount of stopping and starting. Hold a paper towel in your other hand to wipe the tip which collects excess gutta and sometimes picks up fabric lint. Start at the top of your design and work down, being sure to keep your hands, elbows, and clothing out of the wet resist. If you must stop work for a short period of time, put a thin wire or a straight

12-2 Different colors of gutta can be used in one work to give more line variety and emphasis. Detail of **Night Threads #2** by Carolyn Dahl.

the dilutent a little at a time, testing the gutta's consistency on scrap fabric until it flows smoothly. If you add too much, leave the cap off the gutta serti until some of the solvent evaporates, which may take a day. Gutta serti does not penetrate heavy silks very well, and you may need to go over the lines on the reverse side of the fabric, apply a wider line, or use a thinner solution.

pin into the hole so the gutta won't clog the opening.

When you finish your work for the day, pour the remaining gutta serti back into the original bottle, clean out the squeeze bottle, and flush the nib with solvent. Allow the gutta serti to dry on the fabric, usually overnight.

Applying Gutta Serti with a Paper Cone

A paper cone, much like a pastry cone for cake decorating, can also be used to apply the gutta serti. A 4" x 6" square of heavy tracing paper, or vellum, is rolled into a cone with the tip in the center of the longest side. Roll the paper tightly, so there's barely a hole in the tip, or none at all. Place a piece of tape over the paper overlaps and around the body of the cone.

Hold the cone upright and fill approximately half full or less with the gutta serti. Carefully fold the top over two or three times to close, and secure with tape so the gutta can't escape when pressure is applied to the cone. If your cone rolling was perfect, you will need to make a tiny hole in the tip with a pin, or snip off a miniscule piece at a slant with a razor blade. Most of the time though, a very small hole will already be present. Don't cut off anything until you've drawn on some test fabric. Usually the existing hole is suffi-

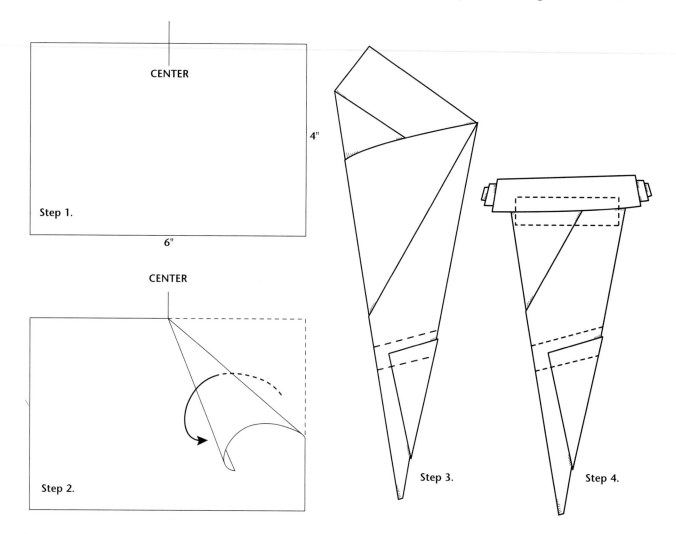

Fig. 12-1 Making a paper cone for gutta serti: Step 1. Cut a piece of heavy tracing paper 4" x 6". Locate the center of the longest side. Step 2. Begin rolling the paper, keeping the tip at the center. Roll tightly to make a very fine tip. Step 3. Wrap a piece of tape around the cone to secure the paper overlap. Fill the cone ½ full with gutta serti. Step 4. Roll down the top of cone and close securely with tape to prevent gutta leakage. Cut a tiny amount off the tip if necessary.

12-3 Detail of *"Jungle Flower"* by Carolyn Dahl, a commission for Tiffany and Co.

12-4 Placing the dye at the top of the flower petals causes it to bleed downward, but stop before it totally colors the shape. Detail of **Iris Garden** by Carolyn Dahl, a commission for Tiffany and Co.

ciently large. Gently squeeze the cone and the gutta will start to flow. Hold the cone in a fairly vertical position and draw it gently across the fabric, moving slowly.

Although it may sound more difficult than using a plastic squeeze bottle, the cone has several advantages: a very fine line can be drawn, unused gutta can be left in the cone in a plastic bag as there are no nibs to clog, and fewer bubbles occur because the cone doesn't suck in air like a plastic bottle when you release the pressure. Best of all, no clean up is required as the used cones can be discarded. I also find that if I am drawing a very complex pattern that may take most of the day to complete, the cone doesn't tire my hand muscles as much as a squeeze bottle.

Water-Soluble Gutta

If you do not chose to use the traditional gutta serti, many water-soluble guttas, or resists, are available in ready-to-use plastic bottles. Unlike gutta serti, water-soluble resists can be removed with water, but that also means they can be washed off the fabric with any water, including dyes. Thus some precautions must

be followed to prevent the dyes from dissolving the resist lines.

Before beginning your design transfer, test your brand of resist on the fabric you intend to use. Most water-soluble resists were developed to be used with particular dyes or fabric paints. As we are substituting fiber reactive dye solutions that contain auxillary chemicals, always do a test strip to be sure that the resist you've chosen will create a strong barrier. I have had good results with Sabra silk resist (PRO Chemical and Dye), which can be colored with the dyes, but many others will work successfully also.

Use only lightweight silks and allow the resist to dry completely before painting. Many instructions say that the silk may be painted while the resist is still wet, but it doesn't work well for me. Either the dye breaks through the moist line, or I smear it with my brush.

When painting, do not overload the brush and flood the fabric with liquid. Paint in a rather dry style, applying the color to the center of the shape and allowing it to bleed to the resist line. Avoid painting over the lines, as the liquid may weaken the resist and cause feathering.

12-5 The shapes within the purple nasturtium flower were created by painting a second color over a dried color. Before the dye is set, color can be moved or textured with another color, or with chemical water. Detail of **Nasturtium,** by Carolyn Dahl, a commission for Tiffany and Co.

The fabrics may be heat set with an iron, dryer, or steam. I would, however, avoid batch setting as the lengthened exposure to moisture could cause some line edges to erode and allow the dye to seep into reserved areas.

If you are ever in doubt as to whether the product you are about to purchase is a solvent or water-based resist, read the label for the removal process. If it can be rinsed out, it's a water-soluble resist.

PAINTING TECHNIQUES

As liquid dye is similar to other water media, many of the silk painting techniques are derived from watercolor methods. As you apply the liquid color to the silk, you will begin to understand why the following are silk painters' favorite techniques.

Touch a loaded brush to the center of a shape and let the dye spread and lighten as it rushes to the edge.

Paint a shape with a color, allow it to dry, and then touch areas with a second color or pure chemical water. Wherever you place the new color or the water, you'll get nice color blooms. Paint a shape and then blot or rub out the center to give two different values of the same color. Fill a background space with chemical water first, and then add colors for a softly blended quality. Or paint just one side of a shape and let the dye run to the other side growing lighter as it progresses.

One of the harder techniques to achieve in silk painting is a smooth background, free of stop and start lines. As most silk designs are more complex, going around the many shapes at a quick pace can be a real challenge.

Start by mixing a sufficient quantity of

12-6 A mixture of salt crystals placed at the same time on the fabric create their own composition of pulled patterns.

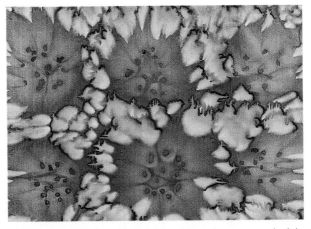

12-7 Rock salt placed inside the shapes leaves wonderful dark crystal patterns on the silk.

dye so you don't run out. Select the largest brush possible. Work in one direction trying to end each pass at the selvage and not in the center of the fabric. Keep the edges wet and work quickly. If you do get a hard edge rub it immediately, which will often blend it or at least make it less conspicuous.

SALT EFFECTS

Salt patterns on silk have almost become the silk painters' trademark. Although the patterns look complex and time consuming, the process is fairly simple. The salt is placed on the fabric while the dye is wet. As the salt absorbs liquid from the surrounding area, the color is pulled into distinctive patterns. Even though the actual process may be easy, some factors influence the salt's effectiveness and the final results.

Fabric and Color

One of the reasons habutai silk is so often used in silk painting is that it yields beautiful salt patterns. Heavier silks and cotton can also be used, but the results are not as dramatic. White or light pastel colored fabrics should be selected so the pulling action can be clearly seen. The fabric should be stretched tightly over a frame while painting and salting, so the dye doesn't pool in low spots and dissolve the salt.

Certain colors and intensities react best with the salt. Dark-to-medium values of forest green, purple, teal blue, raspberry or magenta, navy blue, and some browns create strong patterns. Pastel dye colors produce a very subtle pattern as the values between the area around the salt crystal and the areas from which the color was pulled lack much contrast.

Salt Type and Placement

Salt comes in various crystal sizes. Each will give a slightly different effect depending on its size, additives, and impurities. Experiment with whatever type you find: uniodized table salt, coarse Kosher salt, rock salt (used for making ice cream), canning and pickling salt, and water softener salts. The most frequently used salt is regular table salt which has a smaller crystal and yields a feathery pattern. Avoid iodized salt as iodine is a metal that can dull the dye's color. Although rock salt has impurities that can also affect the color, I still use it because its large crystal size is perfect for some patterns.

To understand how each crystal reacts with your fabric, make a salt sampler. Stretch the fabric on a frame and draw large squares with the gutta. Try a different color and salt in each square. Use only a few grains for a widely spaced pattern and then try densely packed crystals for a spotted mass. Once you know what each crystal type does on your

12-9 A salt patterned background adds depth to a simple flower image.

12-10 In a complex design, salt is best used to highlight certain areas. In this detail from **Space Stream #1**, the circles have been salted to create a texture that contrasts with the smooth background. Silkwork by Carolyn Dahl.

fabric, you can decide if you want an allover sprinkling of one salt, or hand placing of individual chunks, or a mixture of salts for an interactive pattern.

Moisture in the Fabric and the Salt

Only experience and observation will tell you exactly when to drop the salt onto the wet fabric. If you add the salt too soon after painting, it will dissolve in the excess moisture. If you wait too long, the dye locks into the fibers and the salt will be unable to move it.

Watch for the moment that the fabric's sheen changes from the look of water to simply being wet, then act quickly. If in doubt, salt sooner rather than later. When I'm doing large areas of color, such as backgrounds, I paint with my right hand and immediately salt with my left. The reason is that when the dye isn't contained within gutta boundaries, it disperses and dries more quickly, so I have to work even faster.

While the fabric must be wet, the salt must be completely dry if it is to move the color by absorption. Salt is hygroscopic and will collect moisture from the environment, so always store the salt you intend to use for dyeing in a dry place. Before beginning to work, hold it in your hand to determine if it is moist. If so, put it in a shallow pan in a warm oven until dry.

Removing Salt

Allow the salt to dry on the fabric undisturbed. Be sure that it is completely dry before attempting to remove the remaining salt crystals, but don't wait too long or they will become crusty and difficult to remove.

Invert the frame over a large garbage can or a layer of newspapers to collect the dye-stained salt. Shake or lightly tap the backside of the stretched fabric, which will cause most of the crystals to pop off. Avoid brushing the salt crystals across the fabric with your hand. If one crystal still retains moisture, you could streak your fabric with unwanted color.

Hold your frame at an angle. Any glint of light could indicate crystals still stuck to the fabric. Remove remaining salt with a soft bristle brush or your fingernails, or by a gentle rubbing with a scrap piece of clean silk fabric which won't abrade the surface. Try to remove as much salt as possible before the fabric is heat set. The fabric will feel very stiff where the salt has been, but the softness will return after washing.

Setting Salt-Patterned Fabric

Because the pattern is achieved by allowing the salt to dry at its own pace, setting by batching should be avoided as it would interfere with the salt's natural timing. Thus, salt-patterned fabrics should be heat set by ironing or steaming.

If steaming, some precautions should be taken to avoid the problems salt can create in the moisture-filled environment of a steamer. Even though your fabric will be completely dry and all visible traces of salt removed, the areas where the salt was will still contain some residue.

As the steam surrounds the fabric, the remaining salt will attract moisture. Your colors could run or bleed through the protective paper wrap and onto other areas of the fabric. To prevent this, always put an additional layer or two of paper over the salted areas before rolling up the bundle for steaming.

CLOSING

For all the wonders of technology, I believe there will always be a place for hand-designed fabric and those who produce it. If you hold commercial fabric in one hand and your hand-dyed fabric in the other, only one will have a heartbeat. Somehow for all their efficiency and innovation, machines still can't speak to whatever it is in us that makes us human. Fabric filled with the mark of a soul and the mark of a hand will always be important, no matter how far the definition of fabric stretches.

Footnotes

CHAPTER ONE: THE CLOTH

1. Gaffey, Theresa. "Cotton," *Flying Needle,* February 1993.

2. Ibid

3. Ibid.

4. Feltwell, Dr. John. *The Story of Silk.* New York: St. Martin's Press Inc. 1990.

5. Ibid.

6. Ibid.

7. Ibid.

8. Kolander, Cheryl. *A Silk Worker's Notebook.* Colorado: Interweave Press, Inc., 1985.

9. Nuttall, CarolAnne. "Beginning With Raw Silk," *Shuttle, Spindle and Dyepot.* Vol. XXVI, No. 1, Issue 101, Winter 94-95.

10. Wingate, Isabel B. *Textile Fabrics and Their Selection. New Jersey:* Prentice-Hall Inc., 1964.

11. Recipe for washing with Synthrapol from PRO Chemical and Dye

12. Wingate, Isabel B. *Textile Fabrics and Their Selection.* New Jersey: Prentice-Hall Inc., 1964.

CHAPTER TWO: THE COLORANTS

1. Robinson, Stuart. *A History of Dyed Textiles.* Great Britain: Studio Vista Limited, 1969.

2. Sandburg, Gosta. I*ndigo Textiles, Technique and History.* North Carolina: Lark Books, 1989.

3. Tompson, Frances and Tony. *Synthetic Dyeing.* Newton Abbot Devon: David and Charles Craft Book, 1987.

4. Ibid.

5. Brusatin, Manlio. *A History of Colors.* Massachusetts: Shambhala Publications Inc. 1991.

6. Most dyeing procedures originally came from our chemistry trained suppliers, which is why the basic formulas remain similar from one dyeing book to the next. However, many recipes have been varied by creative artists to fit their working environment, process innovations, and personal experience.

   The procedures presented in this chapter have been reviewed by Don Wiener (PRO Chemical and Dye Inc.) for technical accuracy. If you decide to modify the recipes, be sure you understand how the changes will affect the dyeing chemistry. If in doubt, your supplier will be able to advise you as most have many years of industrial dyeing experience.

7. Books on color: *The Art of Color* by Johannes Itten, *Blue and Yellow Don't Make Green* by Michael Wilcox, *A Color Notation* by A.H. Munsell, and *Interaction of Color* by Josef Albers. Many watercolor books are also excellent for color mixing ideas as watercolor and dyes are both transparent mediums.

CHAPTER 4: BLENDED COLOR PATTERNS

1. Ferron, Miquel. *Airbrush Painting.* New York: Watson-Guptill, 1988.

2. Preval® Paint Sprayers. Precision Valve Corporation, Preval Sprayer Division, P.O. Box 309, Yonkers, NY 10702

CHAPTER FIVE: NATURE'S PATTERNS

1. Little, Robert W. *Nature Printing.* Pennsylvania: Pickwick-Morecraft, Inc. 1984.

2. Hochberg, F.G. "Gyotax," Nature Printing Society Newsletter, Vol. XIII, #1, March 1990.

3. For more information on workshops, conferences, and membership contact: The Nature Printing Society, Santa Barbara Museum of Natural History, 2559 Puesta del Sol Road, Santa Barbara, CA 93105 or Sonja Larsen, 7675 Interlachen Road, Lake Shore, MN 56468.

4. Information taken from the brochure of Screen Process Mfg. Co., the supplier of Inkodyes.

CHAPTER SEVEN: COMPRESSION DYEING

1. Wada, Yoshiko; Mary Kellogg Rice; and Jane Barton. *Shibori, The Inventive Art of Japanese Shaped Resist Dyeing.* New York: Kodansha International/USA Ltd., 1983.

If you have difficulty finding this book call:

Hard-To-Find Needlework Books 617-969-0942

Unicorn Books (800) 289-9276

CHAPTER EIGHT: HEAT TRANSFER DYES

1. Scott, Guy. *Transfer Printing onto Man-Made Fibers.* Massachusetts: Charles T. Branford. Co., 1977.

CHAPTER TEN: DESTRUCTION PATTERNS

1. Robinson, Stuart. *A History of Dyed Textiles.* London: Studio Vista Limited, 1969.

CHAPTER ELEVEN: WAX PATTERNS

1. Anderson, F. *Tie-dyeing and Batik,* London: Octopus Books, 1974.

2. Kretvitsky, Nik. *Batik Art and Craft* New York: Van Nostrand-Reinhold Co. No date found.

3. Singer, Margo and Mary Spyrou. *Textile Arts Multicultural Traditions.* Pennsylvania: Chilton Book Co., 1989.

4. Belfer, Nancy. *Designing In Batik and Tie Dye.* Massachusetts: Davis Publications, Inc., 1972.

5. Anderson, F. Ibid.

6. Tortora, Phyllis G. *Understanding Textiles.* New York: Macmillan Publishing Co., 1987.

7. I have enjoyed these drumming and percussion tapes. *Bones* by Gabrielle Roth and the Mirrors; *Thunderdrums* by Scott Fitzgerald; and any Mickey Hart tape.

8. For information on how to turn any image into a repeat pattern, refer to these textile design books: *Design Your Own Repeat Patterns,* V. Ann Waterman, Dover Publications; and *Textile Print Design,* Richard Fisher and Dorothy Wolfthal, Fairchild Publications.

CHAPTER TWELVE: SILK PAINTING

1. Brown, Gail, *Sensational Silk,* Oregon: Palmer/Pletsch Associates, 1982.

2. Arrants, Cheryl with Jan Asbjornsen *Sew Wonderful Silk,* Seattle: Sew Wonderful, 1980.

3. *The Art of Painting on Silk Vol. 3 Fashions,* Kent: Search Press Ltd. 1990 (no author found).

4. Wingate, Isabel B., *Textile Fabrics and Their Selection.* New Jersey: Prentice-Hall, Inc. 1964.

5. Kennedy, Jill and Jane Varall, *Painting On Silk.* London: Drayad Press Ltd., 1988.

Supply Sources

DYES, PAINTS, GENERAL SUPPLIES

PRO Chemical and Dye Inc.
P.O. Box 14, Somerset MA 02726
(800) 2-BUY-DYE

Dharma Trading Co.
P.O. Box 150916, San Rafael CA 94915
(800) 542-5227 (Versatex)

Rupert, Gibbon and Spider, Inc.
P.O. Box 425, Healdsburg, CA 95448
(800) 442-0455 (Jacquard colors)

Createx/Color Craft
14 Airport Park Rd. East Granby, CT 06026
(800) 243-2712

HEAT TRANSFER DYES

Comotion
2165 N. Forbes Blvd., Tucson, AZ. 85745
(520) 624-3232
(transfer ink stamp pads)

Ranger Industries
15 Park Rd., Tinton Falls, NJ 07724
(908) 389-3535
(stamp pad refill bottles)

Decart Inc., P.O. Box 309, Morrisville, VT
05661, (802) 888-4217
(Deka IronOn paint)

Sax Arts and Crafts
P.O. Box 51710, New Berlin, WI 53151
(800) 558-6696
(Design-Dye heat transfer papers)

HELIOTROPIC (INKODYES)

Screen Process Supplies Mfg. Co.
530 MacDonald Ave., Richmond CA 94801
(510) 235-8330

STENCILS

The Stencil Company
28 Castlewood Dr., Cheektowaga, NY 14227
(716) 656-9430

FABRICS

Testfabrics
P.O. Box 420
Middlesex, NJ 08846
(908) 469-6446
(ready-to-dye fabrics)

Thai Silks
252 State Street, Los Altos, CA 94022
(800) 722-Silk outside CA, or (800) 221-SILK in
CA

SHINSHI AND ORIENTAL SUPPLIES

John Marshall: Works in Fabric
2422 East 23rd St. Oakland CA 94601
(510) 533-8056

RUBBER STAMPS AND SUPPLIES

All Night Media, Inc.
Box 10607, San Rafael CA 94912
(415) 459-3013

California Rubber Stamp Co.
5450 Alhambra Ave., Los Angeles CA 90032
(800) 274-6789
(makes stamps from your designs)

Clearsnap
P.O. Box 98, Anacortes, WA 98221
(800) 448-4862 (PenScore)

Fred Mullet Stamps
2707 59th SW, Suite A, Seattle WA 98116
(206) 932-9482

Fruit Basket Upset
Box 23129, Seattle WA 98102

Galactic Graphic
P.O. Box 238, Ft. Wingate NM 87316

Good Stamps
56 So. Main St., Willits CA 95490
(707) 459-9124

Gumbo Graphics
P.O. Box 11801, Eugene, OR 97440

Hampton Art Stamps
19 Industrial Blvd., Medford NY 11763
(800) 229-1019

Hot Potatoes
2109 Grantland Ave., Nashville TN 37204
(615) 269-0047
(nice fabric stamps)

Inkadinkado
60 Cummings Park, Woburn MA 01801
(800) 888-4652

Ken Brown Stamps
P.O. 567, Academy Avenue
Saxtons River, VT 05154
(802) 869-2622

Meer Image
P.O. Box 12, Arcata, CA 95521
(great bugs)

Moe Wubba
P.O. Box 9121, San Rafael, CA 94912

Pelle's Stamps
P.O. Box 242, Davenport, CA 95017
(408) 425-4743

P.O. Box Rubberstamps
244 W. 19th St., Houston, TX 77008
(713) 864-0656

Posh Impressions
30100 Town Center Dr.
Laguna Niguel, CA 92677
(800) 421-Posh

Rubber Stampede
P.O. Box 246, Berkeley, CA 94701
(800) 546-6888

Stamp Oasis
4750 W. Sahara Ave., Las Vegas, NV 89102
(800) 234-TREK

Stampendous, Inc.
1357 South Lewis Street
Anaheim, CA 92805
(714) 563-9501

The Stamp Pad Co., Inc.
P.O. Box 43, Big Lake, MN 55309
(800) 634-3717

MAGAZINES
Eraser Carvers Quarterly
205 Myron Rd., Syracuse, NY 13219
(self-published)

Fiberarts
50 College St.
Asheville, NC 28801
(704) 253-0457

Rubberstampmadness,
408 SW Monroe #210 Corvallis, OR 97330
(503) 752-0075

Surface Design Journal
P.O. Box 20799
Oakland, CA 94620
(510) 841-2008

STAMP MATERIALS
(rubber blocks, flexible printing plates, carving tools)
NASCO
901 Janesville Ave., P.O. Box 901
Fort Atkinson, WI 53538
(414) 563-2446

United Supply Co.
P.O. Box 9219
Fort Wayne, IN 46899
(800) 322-3247

Sax Arts and Crafts
2405 South Calhoun Rd.
P.O. Box 51710
New Berlin, WI 53151
(414) 784-6880

TEXTILE MARKERS
Sulky of America
3113-D Broadpoint Dr.
Harbor Heights, FL 33983
(800) 874-4115
(heat transfer pens)

Yasutomo & Company
490 Eccles Ave.
South San Francisco, CA 94080
(800) 262-6454
(FabricMate markers)

EK Success
611 Industrial Rd.
Carlstadt, NJ 07072
(800) 524-1349
(ZIG textile markers)

Marvy/Uchida
1027 East Burgrove St.
Carson, CA 90746
(310) 632-0333
(The Fabric Marker)

DEVORÉ SUPPLIES/FABRICS
Silkpaint Corporation
P.O. 18220 Waldron Drive
Waldron, MO 64092
(816) 891-7774
and 47-194 Kamehameha Highway
Kaneohe, HI 96744
(808) 239-9299

Whaleys's of Bradford Ltd.
Harris Court. Great Horton, Bradford,
West Yorkshire, BD7 4EQ, England
(azeta fabric for devoré)

FREE MOTION DARNING FOOT
Little Foot Ltd.
605 Bledsoe N.W. Albuquerque, NM 87107
(525) 345-7647
(Big Foot darning foot works well over painted fabric)

A

Activator mixture 14, 17, 18, 23
Adams, Ann 132
Air Pen 115
Alkali activators 14, 15, 17, 18, 21
Animal/sea sponges 65
Atmospheric color 31
Auchard, Betty 48, 49, 52
Azeta cloth 113, 114

B

Background, painting 142, 145
Barren, for leaf printing 52
Batch setting/batching 18, 142, 145
Batik 116, 118, 123, 124,
Belfer, Nancy 124
Bicarbonate of soda (baking soda) 14, 17, 18, 23, 115, 123
Binding and dyeing 77–79
Black-and-white transformations 28–33
Blended color patterns 34–43
Boser, Brett 93
Braiding and dyeing 73–77, 112

C

Cellulose sponges 65, 66, 70
Chardonnet, Count Hilaire de 9
Chemical water 15, 16, 22, 23, 36, 142
Chrysalis dreams 7
Chiffon 9
China silk 20, 22, 57, 138
Chlorine bleach 11, 109, 111
Clothes dryer setting 19
Colorants 12–27, 60, 89–97, 148
  dyes 9, 12–23, 27, 29–33, 69, 79, 81, 96, 103, 108, 115, 127, 137, 141, 148
  fabric paint 6, 12–14, 23–27, 29, 31, 40, 49–52, 55, 57, 69, 71, 90, 98, 100, 105, 114, 115, 141
  history 13

Color band technique 31, 32
Coloring book 29
Color blotches technique 33
Color mixing 17, 60
Color washes technique 34–38
Compression dyeing 72–85,
  binding 72, 77–79
  braiding 72–77
  knotting 72, 77–79
  scrunching 72, 79–80
  stitching 72, 81–85
  twisting 72, 75–78
Cotton 2, 4, 5, 9, 14, 17, 18, 20, 21, 24, 25, 27, 28, 37, 43, 45, 46, 51, 54, 56, 57, 60, 61, 66, 73, 82, 88, 92, 94, 98, 104, 106, 109, 111, 113–116, 143, 148
  history 2
  purchasing 4, 27
  washing/storing 11, 18, 21, 27, 37, 46, 80, 106, 111
Crazy quilts 5
Crepe de Chine 138
Cultivated caterpillars 6
Custom color mixing 17, 60

D

Dahl, Carolyn 3, 4, 21, 23, 25, 26, 35, 39, 43, 52, 62, 64, 67, 72, 73, 77, 80, 86, 93, 95, 99, 106, 116, 122, 127, 128, 135, 136, 141, 142, 144, 145, 153
Dauber 57, 66, 100
Deka IronOn paint 95–97, 148
Divine threads 9
Design-Dye sheets 94–96
Destruction patterns 106–115, 149
Divine worm 6
Devoré/Burn-out 113
Direct application 14–16, 74
Discharge agent 109
Dispersed dyes 87, 88
Dobbins, Margaret Scott 12, 23
Douppioni silk 138
Dry cleaning 127
Dunnewold, Jane 103
Dye disposal 23

Dyes 2, 3, 9, 12–23, 24, 27, 29, 33, 36, 37, 40, 52, 69, 74, 75, 79, 81, 84, 87–94, 96, 97, 103, 108, 111, 115, 119, 127, 136, 137, 141, 148
  Fiber reactive 3, 9, 14–18, 21–23, 36, 37, 40, 52, 60, 74, 75, 84, 111, 116, 119, 136, 141
  French dyes 136
  Heat transfer dyes 86–97
  Inkodyes 49, 59–63, 148
  Vat dyes 13, 60

E

Erasers, carving 104
Extender 27, 51, 60

F

Fabric paints 6, 12–14, 23–27, 29, 31, 49–51, 69, 71, 90, 105, 141
Fallert, Caryl Bryer 37
Farm-Heumann, Susan 98, 105
Felt, for stamps 129–131
Fiber-Etch 113–115
Fiber reactive dyes 3, 9, 14–18, 21–23, 36, 37, 40, 52, 74, 75, 84, 111, 116, 119, 136 141
  MX and H series 14, 15
  Recipes 16–18, 21–23
    alkali activation 17, 18
    chemical water 16
    mixing dyes 16, 17
    setting dyes 18–20
    thickened dyes 21–23
Fish Printing/Gyotaku 53–58
  direct 54, 55
  indirect 57
Fixer 17
Flexible printing plate 100–103
Formosul 109
French dyes 136

G

Gather, stitch and dye 83
Gutta 19, 121, 136, 139–141
Gyotaku 53, 55–57

H

Habutai silk 138, 143
Harite, how to make 124–125
Heated-foam sponge
    printing 66, 67, 70, 71
Heat setting 18
Heat transfer/dispersed
    dyes 58, 86–97, 148
    dye-saturated sheets 94
    ink stamp pads 88
    powdered dyes 97
    transfer paint 96
    transfer pens 93
    wax transfer crayons 92
Heliotropic (Inkodye)
    printing 59–61, 63

I

Indonesia 81, 121, 123
Inkodyes 49, 59–63, 148
Ironing 18, 24, 83, 90, 92, 96,
    114, 115, 121, 126, 127,
    145
Iron setting 18, 88

J

Jacquard silk fabric 138
Japan 2, 6, 13, 40, 53, 57, 72,
    73, 103, 124, 125, 148
Jetton, Mark 89
Johnson, Melody 36, 42
Jolly, Jean Batiste 127

K

Knotting and dyeing 77–79
Kuhn, Renita 103

L

Leaf printing 48–52, 112
Leaf transfer 94
Lee, Iris 113, 115
Lindveit, Winnie 53, 56
Linear bleed technique 31
Ludigol 22

M

Machado, Ann Bae 53, 57
Machine washing silk 11
Markers, textile 49, 52, 60, 93,
    94, 100, 149

Mercerization 4
Moldable foam (PenScore) 67,
    70, 71
Mommie, silk weight 138
Mullet, Fred 57, 58, 148

N

Needlepoint canvas 64, 99
Neutralizer for bleach 110–112
Newspaper stencils 40
Noil silk 138

P

Painting techniques 28, 48,
    142
Painting the braid 74
Painting the fabric 125
Paper cone for gutta 140
Paper, heat transfer 88, 90
Paraffin 121, 132
Paste, dye 22, 23, 75
Pasteur, Louis 9
Pattern, random and repeat
    100–102, 130
Peel, Charlotte 134
PenScore 66, 67, 71
Perkin, William Henry 13
Photograms 59, 61, 63
Photograph/photocopy
    transfer 94–96, 104–105
Plasse, De Noel 87
Polystyrene foam printing 103
Pongee silk 10, 138
Preparing fabric 10
Presoak, in alkali 17, 18, 40,
    75
Preval sprayers 40
Purchasing cotton 4
Purchasing rayon 9
Procion® MX series 14
Procion® H series 15

R

Rain patterning 44–47
Rayon 2, 9–10, 14, 18, 21, 60,
    61, 73, 109, 113–116
Ready-to-dye fabric 11, 148
Recipes for watercolor effects
    16
Recipes for thickened dye
    effect 21

Resists 19, 112, 115, 121, 138-
    141
Rinsing fabric 11, 15, 17, 18,
    21, 80, 111, 112
Rubber blocks for stamps 104
Ruzich, Cheri 44, 46, 47

S

Safety precautions 15, 109
Salt effects 143-145
Sawyer, Renata 52
Scheele, Carl William 109
Scrunching and dyeing 79
Selective focus technique 33
Self-designed stamps 70,
    98–105
    erasers 103, 104
    flexible printing plate 100,
        102, 103
    rubber blocks 104, 105
    sheet foam 103
Setting dyes (see fiber reac-
    tive) 18
Sharp, Kate 93
Sharp, Lisa 25, 39, 116
Sheet foam for stamps 103
Shibori 72, 73, 80
Shinshi 125, 126, 148
Silk, artificial 9
Silk painting 17, 53, 121,
    136–145
Silk, sericulture 6, 7, 9
Silk, types of 5, 22, 138
Silk, washing 10, 11, 21, 27,
    34, 37, 145
Silken cloaks 7
Silkworms 6
Sodium alginate, thickener
    22, 109
Sodium bisulfate for devoré
    113–115
Sodium bisulfate, neutralizer
    110
Sodium carbonate (washing
    soda, soda ash, sal soda,
    fixer) 17
Sodium hexametaphosphate,
    water softener 16,22
Sponged patterns 58, 64,
    68–70
Spray dyeing 38–43

Stamps 57, 58, 87–92, 94, 98–105, 129–135, 148
  self-designed stamps 70, 98–105
Steam setting 18–20, 127, 145
  canning pot steamer 19
  vertical steamer 20
Stencil 30, 40, 43, 59, 70, 84–86
  definition 40
  newspaper 40, 41
Stitch-and-dye technique 81–84
Stretching fabric 125, 126
Sublistatic/sublimation 87
Sulky IronOn pens 93, 94
Supply sources 148
Synthetic fabric 2, 14, 87
Synthrapol 10, 21
  rinsing agent 21
  scouring agent before dyeing 10
  sun reactive dyes 59

T
Testfabrics 11, 37, 45, 148
Texture cubes 90, 91, 95
Thickened dye recipes 21
Thiourea dioxide, bleach 109
Tiny grains 6
Tjanting tools 118, 120, 121, 123, 124
Transferring drawing to cloth 119

Tritik 81
Twisting and dyeing 77–79

U
Ultraviolet light/sun lamps 5, 60, 63
Urea pellets 16

V
Vat dyes 13, 60

W
Wada, Yoshiko, Mary Kellog Rice, Jane Barton 73, 147
Washing cotton 10
Washing rayon 11
Washing silk 10
Washing soda, alkali 17, 75
Water softener (Calgon, Metaphos) 16, 22, 143
Wax crayons for heat transfer 92
Wax patterns 116–136
Wax removal 19, 126–128
Wax resist 112, 116, 121, 123, 124, 127–129, 133, 134
  safety 121
  types
    batik wax 121
    beeswax 121
    mycrocrystalline 121
    paraffin 121
Wax stamping 129–135

precut wood stamps 100, 130, 134
Weighted silks 5
Wheel stamps 90, 91
White moths 9
Willey, Mary Ann 81, 130
Wingate, Isabel 138

Z
Zig textile markers 52, 149

Carolyn Dahl's first career was in theater as a professional singer and actress. Many of the dyeing and painting techniques she loves were first encountered in stage construction and costuming courses at the University of Minnesota. Her career turned toward the graphic arts after ten years of performing in musicals, industrial films, commercials, summer stock, and off-Broadway productions.

After attending art schools in New York, California, and Florence, Italy, she chose dyed and painted textiles and paper vessels/baskets as her career focus. Over the years, her work has been shown in many museums and art centers; in numerous commercial galleries throughout the United States; and in Holland, and Italy. Magazines such as *American Craft, Fiberarts, House Beautiful, Southwest Art, Surface Design Journal, Architecture Minnesota, Quilting Today,* and *Better Homes and Gardens Quilting Ideas* have featured her work.

Four books, including *Fiberarts Design Books Three* and *Five*, have published Ms. Dahl's dyed textiles. Her colorful paper vessels/baskets can be seen in *Papermaking in Basketry* (Lark Books), *Basketry Roundup* Vol. 1 & 2 (Press de La Plantz), *Paper Sculpture* (Davis Books), and *The Guild 7* in which she was an American Crafts Award winner.

In addition to producing artwork in her Houston studio, Ms. Dahl also travels frequently as a lecturer and teacher at fiber conferences around the country.

Photo by Aileen Guggenheim

AQS BOOKS ON QUILTS

This is only a partial listing of the books on quilts that are available from the American Quilter's Society. AQS books are known the world over for their timely topics, clear writing, beautiful color photographs, and accurate illustrations and patterns. The following books are available from your local bookseller, quilt shop, or public library. If you are unable to locate certain titles in your area, you may order by mail from the AMERICAN QUILTER'S SOCIETY, P.O. Box 3290, Paducah, KY 42002-3290. Add $2.00 for postage for the first book ordered and 40¢ for each additional book. Include item number, title, and price when ordering. Allow 14 to 21 days for delivery. Customers with Visa, MasterCard, or Discover may phone in orders from 7:00–5:00 CST, Monday–Friday, Toll Free 1-800-626-5420.

4595	**Above & Beyond Basics,** Karen Kay Buckley	$18.95
2282	**Adapting Architectural Details for Quilts,** Carol Wagner	$12.95
4813	**Addresses & Birthdays,** compiled by Klaudeen Hansen **(HB)**	$14.95
4543	**American Quilt Blocks: 50 Patterns for 50 States,** Beth Summers	$16.95
4696	**Amish Kinder Komforts,** Bettina Havig	$14.95
4829	**Anita Shackelford: Surface Textures,** Anita Shackelford **(HB)**	$24.95
4899	**Appliqué Paper Greetings,** Elly Sienkiewicz **(HB)**	$24.95
3790	**Appliqué Patterns from Native American Beadwork Designs,** Dr. Joyce Mori	$14.95
2099	**Ask Helen: More About Quilting Designs,** Helen Squire	$14.95
2207	**Award-Winning Quilts: 1985-1987**	$24.95
2354	**Award-Winning Quilts: 1988-1989**	$24.95
3425	**Award-Winning Quilts: 1990-1991**	$24.95
3791	**Award-Winning Quilts: 1992-1993**	$24.95
4830	**Baskets: Celtic Style,** Scarlett Rose	$19.95
4593	**Blossoms by the Sea: Making Ribbon Flowers for Quilts,** Faye Labanaris	$24.95
4898	**Borders & Finishing Touches,** Bonnie K. Browning	$16.95
4697	**Caryl Bryer Fallert: A Spectrum of Quilts, 1983-1995,** Caryl Bryer Fallert	$24.95
4626	**Celtic Geometric Quilts,** Camille Remme	$16.95
3926	**Celtic Style Floral Appliqué,** Scarlett Rose	$14.95
2208	**Classic Basket Quilts,** Elizabeth Porter & Marianne Fons	$16.95
2355	**Creative Machine Art,** Sharee Dawn Roberts	$24.95
4818	**Dear Helen, Can You Tell Me?** Helen Squire	$15.95
3399	**Dye Painting!** Ann Johnston	$19.95
4814	**Encyclopedia of Designs for Quilting,** Phyllis D. Miller **(HB)**	$34.95
3468	**Encyclopedia of Pieced Quilt Patterns,** compiled by Barbara Brackman	$34.95
3846	**Fabric Postcards,** Judi Warren	$22.95
4594	**Firm Foundations,** Jane Hall & Dixie Haywood	$18.95
4900	**Four Blocks Continued…,** Linda Giesler Carlson	$16.95
2381	**From Basics to Binding,** Karen Kay Buckley	$16.95
4526	**Gatherings: America's Quilt Heritage,** Kathlyn F. Sullivan	$34.95
2097	**Heirloom Miniatures,** Tina M. Gravatt	$9.95
4628	**Helen's Guide to quilting in the 21st century,** Helen Squire	$16.95
1906	**Irish Chain Quilts: A Workbook of Irish Chains,** Joyce B. Peaden	$14.95
3784	**Jacobean Appliqué: Book I, "Exotica,"** Campbell & Ayars	$18.95
4544	**Jacobean Appliqué: Book II, "Romantica,"** Campbell & Ayars	$18.95
3904	**The Judge's Task,** Patricia J. Morris	$19.95
4751	**Liberated Quiltmaking,** Gwen Marston **(HB)**	$24.95
4897	**Lois Smith's Machine Quiltmaking,** Lois Smith	$19.95
4523	**Log Cabin Quilts: New Quilts from an Old Favorite**	$14.95
4545	**Log Cabin with a Twist,** Barbara T. Kaempfer	$18.95
4815	*Love to Quilt:* **Bears, Bears, Bears,** Karen Kay Buckley	$14.95
4833	*Love to Quilt:* **Broderie Perse: The Elegant Quilt,** Barbara W. Barber	$14.95
4598	*Love to Quilt:* **Men's Vests,** Alexandra Capadalis Dupré	$14.95
4816	*Love to Quilt:* **Necktie Sampler Blocks,** Janet B. Elwin	$14.95
4753	*Love to Quilt:* **Penny Squares,** Willa Baranowski	$12.95
4911	**Mariner's Compass Quilts: New Quilts from an Old Favorite**	$16.95
4752	**Miniature Quilts: Connecting New & Old Worlds,** Tina M. Gravatt	$14.95
4514	**Mola Techniques for Today's Quilters,** Charlotte Patera	$18.95
3330	**More Projects and Patterns,** Judy Florence	$18.95
1981	**Nancy Crow: Quilts and Influences,** Nancy Crow	$29.95
3331	**Nancy Crow: Work in Transition,** Nancy Crow	$12.95
4828	**Nature, Design & Silk Ribbons,** Cathy Grafton	$18.95
3332	**New Jersey Quilts,** The Heritage Quilt Project of New Jersey	$29.95
3927	**New Patterns from Old Architecture,** Carol Wagner	$12.95
2153	**No Dragons on My Quilt,** Jean Ray Laury	$12.95
4627	**Ohio Star Quilts: New Quilts from an Old Favorite**	$16.95
3469	**Old Favorites in Miniature,** Tina Gravatt	$15.95
4831`	**Optical Illusions for Quilters,** Karen Combs	$22.95
4515	**Paint and Patches: Painting on Fabrics with Pigment,** Vicki L. Johnson	$18.95
4513	**Plaited Patchwork,** Shari Cole	$19.95
3928	**Precision Patchwork for Scrap Quilts,** Jeannette Tousley Muir	$12.95
4779	**Protecting Your Quilts: A Guide for Quilt Owners, Second Edition**	$6.95
4542	**A Quilted Christmas,** edited by Bonnie Browning	$18.95
2380	**Quilter's Registry,** Lynne Fritz	$9.95
3467	**Quilting Patterns from Native American Designs,** Dr. Joyce Mori	$12.95
3470	**Quilting with Style,** Gwen Marston & Joe Cunningham	$24.95
2284	**Quiltmaker's Guide: Basics & Beyond,** Carol Doak	$19.95
4918	**Quilts by Paul D. Pilgrim: Blending the Old & the New,** Gerald E. Roy	$16.95
2257	*Quilts:* **The Permanent Collection – MAQS**	$9.95
3793	*Quilts:* **The Permanent Collection – MAQS Volume II**	$9.95
3789	**Roots, Feathers & Blooms,** Linda Giesler Carlson	$16.95
4512	**Sampler Quilt Blocks from Native American Designs,** Dr. Joyce Mori	$14.95
3796	**Seasons of the Heart & Home: Quilts for a Winter's Day,** Jan Patek	$18.95
3761	**Seasons of the Heart & Home: Quilts for Summer Days,** Jan Patek	$18.95
2357	**Sensational Scrap Quilts,** Darra Duffy Williamson	$24.95
4783	**Silk Ribbons by Machine,** Jeanie Sexton	$15.95
3929	**The Stori Book of Embellishing,** Mary Stori	$16.95
3903	**Straight Stitch Machine Appliqué,** Letty Martin	$16.95
3792	**Striplate Piecing,** Debra Wagner	$24.95
3930	**Tessellations & Variations,** Barbara Ann Caron	$14.95
3788	**Three-Dimensional Appliqué and Embroidery Embellishment: Techniques for Today's Album Quilt,** Anita Shackelford	$24.95
4596	**Ties, Ties, Ties: Traditional Quilts from Neckties,** Janet B. Elwin	$19.95
3931	**Time-Span Quilts: New Quilts from Old Tops,** Becky Herdle	$16.95
4919	**Transforming Fabric,** Carolyn Dahl	$29.95
2029	**A Treasury of Quilting Designs,** Linda Goodmon Emery	$14.95
3847	**Tricks with Chintz,** Nancy S. Breland	$14.95
2286	**Wonderful Wearables: A Celebration of Creative Clothing,** Virginia Avery	$24.95
4812	**Who's Who in American Quilting,** edited by Bonnie Browning **(HB)**	$49.95
4956	**Variegreat! New Dimensions in Traditional Quilts,** Linda Glantz	$19.95
4972	**20th Century Quilts,** Cuesta Benberry and Joyce Gross	$ 9.95